15 MINUTE
FRENCH

DK EYEWITNESS TRAVEL

15-MINUTE
FRENCH

LEARN FRENCH
IN JUST 15
MINUTES A DAY

CAROLINE LEMOINE

DORLING KINDERSLEY

London, New York, Munich, Melbourne, and Delhi

Dorling Kindersley Limited
Senior Editor Angeles Gavira
Project Art Editor Vanessa Marr
DTP Designer John Goldsmid
Production Controller Luca Frassinetti
Publishing Manager Liz Wheeler
Managing Art Editor Philip Ormerod
Publishing Director Jonathan Metcalf
Art Director Bryn Walls

Language content for Dorling Kindersley by
g-and-w publishing

Produced for Dorling Kindersley by
Schermuly Design Co.
Art Editor Hugh Schermuly
Project Editor Cathy Meeus
Special photography Mike Good

First published in Great Britain in 2005 by
Dorling Kindersley Limited
80 Strand, London WC2R 0RL
A Penguin Company

A CIP catalogue record is available for this
book from the British Library
ISBN-13: 978 1 4053 0287 6
ISBN-10: 1 4053 0287 9
15-Minute French is also available in a pack
with two CDs
ISBN-13: 978 1 4053 0971 4
ISBN-10: 1 4053 0971 7
Colour reproduction by Colourscan, Singapore
Printed and bound in China by Leo Paper
Products Limited

See our complete catalogue at
www.dk.com

Contents

How to use this book

This main part of the book is devoted to 12 themed chapters, broken down into five 15-minute daily lessons, the last of which is a revision lesson. So, in just 12 weeks you will have completed the course. A concluding reference section contains a menu guide and English-to-French and French-to-English dictionaries.

Warm up and clock
Each day starts with a one-minute warm up that encourages you to recall vocabulary or phrases you have learned previously. A clock to the right of the heading bar indicates the amount of time you are expected to spend on each exercise.

Instructions
Each exercise is numbered and introduced by instructions that explain what to do. In some cases additional information is given about the language point being covered.

Cultural/Conversational tip
These panels provide additional insights into life in France and language usage.

Text styles
Distinctive text styles differentiate French and English, and the pronunciation guide (see right).

In conversation
Illustrated dialogues reflecting how vocabulary and phrases are used in everyday situations appear throughout the book.

How to use the flap
The book's cover flaps allow you to conceal the French so that you can test whether you have remembered correctly.

Review and repeat
A recap of selected elements of previous lessons helps to reinforce your knowledge.

Pronunciation guide

Many French sounds will already be familiar to you, but a few require special attention. Take note of how these letters are pronounced:

r a French **r** is pronounced in the back of the throat, producing a sound a little like gargling

j a French **j** is soft like the sound in the middle of *pleasure* (as opposed to the hard English *j* as in *major*)

n **n** is pronounced nasally when in the combination **on**, **an** or **in**. Imagine saying *huh* through your nose. The nasal **n** is shown in the pronunciation with this symbol: ñ

ch ch in French is equivalent to *sh* in English, as in *ship*

er/ez these endings are pronounced *ay* as in *play*

Pay attention also to these vowel sounds as they may vary from English:

i as the English *keep*
au as the English *over*
eu as the English *fur*
oi as the English *wag*

Below each French word or phrase you will find a pronunciation transcription. Read this, bearing in mind the tips above, and you will achieve a comprehensible result. But remember that the transcription can only ever be an approximation and that there is no real substitute for listening to and mimicking native speakers.

Useful phrases
Selected phrases relevant to the topic help you speak and understand.

EATING AND DRINKING 19

Useful phrases

Learn these phrases. Read the English under the pictures and say the phrase in French as shown on the right. Then conceal the French with the cover flap and test yourself.

le pain, bien sûr, urgh pañ byañ bread

Je voudrais un grand café, s'il vous plaît.
juh voodray uñ grañ kafay, seel voo play

I'd like a large black coffee, please.

C'est tout?
say too

Is that all?

Je prends un croissant.
juh prañ uñ krwasoñ

I'll have a croissant.

le café au lait?
luh kafay oh lay large coffee with milk

C'est combien?
say koñbyañ

How much is that?

Alors deux croissants. C'est combien?
alor duh krwasoñ. say koñbyañ?

Two croissants, then. How much is that?

Quatre euros, s'il vous plaît.
katr uhroh, seel voo play

Four euros, please.

...ui, bien sûr.
wee, byañ sewr
Yes, certainly.

Say it
In these exercises you are asked to apply what you have learned using different vocabulary.

5 Say it

Do you have a single room?

For six nights.

Does it have a balcony?

Menu guide
Use this guide as a reference for food terminology and popular French dishes.

Dictionary
A mini-dictionary provides ready reference from English to French and French to English for 2,500 words.

132 DICTIONARY

Dictionary
English to French

The gender of a singular French noun is indicated by the word for the: **le** and **la** (masculine and feminine). If these are abbreviated to **l'** in front of a vowel or the letter "h," or if the noun is plural, indicated by **les**, then the gender is indicated by the abbreviations "(m)" or "(f)." French adjectives (adj) vary according to the gender and number of the word they describe; the masculine form is shown here. In most cases, you add an **-e** to the masculine form to make it feminine. Certain endings use a different rule: masculine adjectives that end in **-x** adopt an **-se** ending in the feminine form, while those that end in **-ien** change to **-ienne**. Some feminine adjectives that do not follow these rules are shown here and follow the abbreviation "(fem)." For the plural form, a (plural) **-s** is usually added.

128 MENU GUIDE

Menu guide
This guide lists the most common terms you may encounter on French menus or when shopping for food. If you can't find an exact phrase, try looking up its component parts.

Bonjour
Hello

In France it is part of the culture to greet family and friends with kisses on the cheek. The number of kisses varies from two to four. For example, it is usually three kisses in the south but two in Brittany. In more formal situations, a handshake is part of the normal greeting.

2 Words to remember

Look at these polite expressions and say them aloud. Cover the text on the left with the cover flap and try to remember the French for each item. Check your answers.

Salut!
saloo
Hi!

Bonjour. boñjoor	*Hello.*
Bonsoir/bonne nuit. boñswar/bon nwee	*Good evening/good night.*
Je m'appelle Jean. juh mapell joñ	*My name is Jean.*
Enchanté *(men)/* **Enchantée** *(women).* oñshontay	*Pleased to meet you.*

🇫🇷 **Cultural tip** The French tend to greet people with "monsieur" (sir), "madame" (madam, for older women), or "mademoiselle" (miss, for younger women) much more than most English-speakers would.

3 In conversation: formal

Bonjour. Je m'appelle Céline Legrand.
boñjoor. juh mapell seleen luhgroñ

Hello. My name's Céline Legrand.

Bonjour madame. Monsieur Rossi, enchanté.
boñjoor ma-dam. musyuh rossee, oñshontay

Hello (madam). Mr Rossi, pleased to meet you.

Enchantée.
oñshontay

Pleased to meet you.

4 Put into practice

Join in this conversation. Read the French beside the pictures on the left and then follow the instructions to make your reply. Then test yourself by concealing the answers on the right with the cover flap.

Bonjour monsieur.
boñjoor musyuh.
Hello sir.

Say: Hello mademoiselle.

Bonjour mademoiselle.
boñjoor mad-mwazel

Je m'appelle Martine.
juh mapell marteen.
My name is Martine.

Say: Pleased to meet you.

Enchanté.
oñshontay

5 Useful phrases

Familiarize yourself with these phrases. Read them aloud several times and try to memorize them. Conceal the French with the cover flap and test yourself.

Goodbye.	**Au revoir.** ovwar
See you soon.	**A bientôt.** ah byañtoe
See you tomorrow.	**A demain.** ah dumañ
Thank you (very much).	**Merci (beaucoup).** mairsee (bohkoo)

6 In conversation: informal

Alors, à demain?
alor, ah dumañ

So, see you tomorrow?

Oui, au revoir.
wee, ovwar

Yes, goodbye.

Au revoir. A bientôt.
ovwar. ah byañtoe

Goodbye. See you soon.

1   Warm up

Say "hello" and "goodbye" in French. (pp.8–9)

Now say "My name is..." (pp.8–9)

Say "sir" and "madam". (pp.8–9)

Les relations
Relatives

In French the same word is used for relationships by marriage: **beau-père** means both father-in-law and stepfather, and **belle-fille** means daughter-in-law and stepdaughter. The French for *the* is **le** or **la**, and *a* is **un** or **une**, depending on whether the word is masculine or feminine (see below).

---

2   Match and repeat

Look at the people in this scene and match their numbers with the vocabulary list at the side. Read the French words aloud. Now, cover the list with the flap and test yourself.

1 **le grand-père**
   luh groñpair

2 **le frère**
   luh frair

3 **la sœur**
   lah sur

4 **le père**
   luh pair

5 **la mère**
   lah mair

6 **la grand-mère**
   lah groñmair

7 **le fils**
   luh fees

8 **la fille**
   lah feeyuh

❶ *grandfather*
brother ❷   ❸ *sister*
❹ *father*
❺ *mother*
grandmother ❻   ❼ *son*   ❽ *daughter*

🇫🇷 **Conversational tip** In French, things as well as people are masculine (m) or feminine (f). For example, "wine" is masculine: "*le* vin", but "car" is feminine: "*la* voiture". For the plural **les** is used for both masculine and feminine. In this book "m" or "f" indicates the gender after a plural.

3 Words to remember: relatives

Look at these words and say them aloud. Conceal the text on the right with the cover flap and try to remember the French. Check your answers. Then practise the phrases below.

le mari   **la femme**
luh maree   lah fam
husband   *wife*

Nous sommes mariés.
Noo som mareeay
We are married.

sister-in-law/ stepsister	**la belle-sœur** lah bell sur
brother-in-law/ stepbrother	**le beau-frère** luh boe frair
half-sister	**la demi-sœur** lah dumee sur
half-brother	**le demi-frère** luh dumee frair
children	**les enfants** *(m)* lay zoñfoñ
I have four children.	**J'ai quatre enfants.** jay katruh oñfoñ
I have two stepdaughters.	**J'ai deux belles-filles.** jay duh bell feeyuh

4 Words to remember: numbers

Memorize these words. Now cover the French and test yourself.

Be careful with the pronunciation of **deux** and **trois**. When you say them in front of a word that starts with a vowel, you need to say an extra "z" sound – for example, **deux enfants** (*two children*) is pronounced duh zoñfoñ, and **trois éclairs** (*three eclairs*), trwah zayclair. This is also true of other words.

5 Say it

I have five sons.

I have three sisters and a brother.

I have two stepsons.

one	**un/une** uñ *(m)*/oon *(f)*
two	**deux** duh
three	**trois** trwah
four	**quatre** katruh
five	**cinq** sank
six	**six** sees
seven	**sept** set
eight	**huit** weet
nine	**neuf** nurf
ten	**dix** dees

1 Warm up

Say the French for as
many members of the
family as you can.
(pp.10–11)

Say "I have two sons".
(pp.10–11)

Ma famille
My family

The French have two ways of saying
"you": **vous** for people you meet or
don't know very well and **tu** for
family and friends. Similarly, there are
different words for "your". The words
for "my" and "your" also change
depending on whether they relate to
masculine, feminine, or plural nouns.

2 Words to remember

Say these words out loud a few times. Cover the French with the flap
and try to remember the French word for each item.

mon moñ	*my (with masculine)*
ma mah	*my (with feminine)*
mes may	*my (with plural)*
ton toñ	*your (informal, with masculine)*
ta tah	*your (informal, with feminine)*
tes tay	*your (informal, with plural)*
votre votruh	*your (formal, with masculine or feminine)*
vos voe	*your (formal, with plural)*

Voici mes parents.
vwasee may paroñ
These are my parents.

3 In conversation

**Vous avez des
enfants?**
voo zavay day zoñfoñ

*Do you have any
children?*

Oui, j'ai deux filles.
wee, jay duh feeyuh

*Yes, I have two
daughters.*

**Voici mes filles.
Et vous?**
vwasee may feeyuh.
ay voo

*These are my
daughters. And you?*

Conversational tip The French usually ask a question by simply raising the pitch of the voice at the end of a statement – for example, "Vous voulez un café?" ("Do you want a coffee?"). You could also ask the same question by inverting the verb and subject: "Voulez-vous un café?". Or you can put "Est-ce que" in front of the sentence: "Est-ce que vous voulez un café?"

4 Useful phrases

Read these phrases aloud several times and try to memorize them. Conceal the French with the cover flap and test yourself.

Do you have any brothers? (formal)

Vous avez des frères?
voo zavay day frair

Do you have any brothers? (informal)

Tu as des frères?
tew ah day frair

This is my husband.

Voici mon mari.
vwasee moñ maree

That's my wife.

C'est ma femme.
say mah fam

Is that your sister? (formal)

C'est votre sœur?
say votruh sur

Is that your sister? (informal)

C'est ta sœur?
say tah sur

J'ai un beau-fils.
jay uñ boe fees

I have a stepson.

5 Say it

Do you have any brothers and sisters? (formal)

Do you have any children? (informal)

I have two sisters.

This is my wife.

Say "See you soon".
(pp.8–9)

Say "I am married"
(pp.10–11) and
"I have a daughter".
(pp.12–13)

Etre et avoir
To be and to have

There are some essential verbs for you
to learn in this course. You can use
these to construct a large variety of
useful phrases. The first two are **être**
(*to be*) and **avoir** (*to have*). Learn them
carefully as French verbs change more
than English ones according to the
pronoun (I, you, etc.) used.

2 Etre: to be

Familiarize yourself with the different forms of **être** (*to be*). Use the
cover flaps to test yourself and, when you are confident, practise the
sample sentences below.

je suis juh swee	*I am*
tu es tew ay	*you are (informal singular)*
il/elle est eel/el ay	*he/she is*
nous sommes noo som	*we are*
vous êtes voo zet	*you are (formal singular or plural)*
ils/elles sont eel/el soñ	*they are*

Je suis anglaise.
juh swee zonglayz
I'm English.

Je suis fatigué(e). juh swee fatigay	*I'm tired.*
Vous êtes à l'heure. voo zet ah lur	*You're on time.*
Elle est heureuse? el ay tururz	*Is she happy?*
Nous sommes français. noo som froñsay	*We're French.*

3 Avoir: to have

Practise **avoir** (*to have*) and the sample sentences, then test yourself.

I have	**j'ai** jay
you have (informal singular)	**tu as** tew ah
he/she has	**il/elle a** eel/el ah
we have	**nous avons** noo zavoñ
you have (formal singular or plural)	**vous avez** voo zavay
they have	**ils/elles ont** eel/el zoñ

Il a deux baguettes.
eel ah duh baget
He has two baguettes.

He has a meeting.	**Il a un rendez-vous.** eel ah uñ roñday-voo
Do you have a mobile phone?	**Vous avez un portable?** voo zavay uñ portabluh
How many brothers and sisters do you have?	**Vous avez combien de frères et sœurs?** voo zavay koñbyañ duh frair ay sur

4 Negatives

To make a sentence negative in French, put **ne** in front of the verb and **pas** just after: **nous ne sommes pas anglais** (*we are not English*). If **ne** is followed by a vowel, it becomes **n'**: **je n'ai pas d'enfants** (*I don't have any children*). But many French people drop the **ne** when they're talking, so you'll just hear **nous sommes pas** (*we aren't*), **j'ai pas** (*I haven't*), and so on. Read these sentences aloud, then cover the French with the flap and test yourself.

le vélo
luh vayloe
bicycle

He's not married.	**Il n'est pas marié.** eel nay pah mariyay
I am not sure.	**Je ne suis pas sûr(e).** juh nuh swee pah syur
We don't have any children.	**Nous n'avons pas d'enfants.** noo navoñ pah doñfoñ

Je n'ai pas de voiture.
juh nay pas duh vwatyur
I don't have a car.

Réponses
Answers
Cover with flap

Révisez et répétez
Review and repeat

1 How many?

1 **trois**
trwah

2 **neuf**
nurf

3 **quatre**
katruh

4 **deux**
duh

5 **huit**
weet

6 **dix**
dees

7 **cinq**
sank

8 **sept**
set

9 **six**
sees

1 How many?

Cover the answers with the flap. Then say these French numbers out loud. Check you have remembered the French correctly.

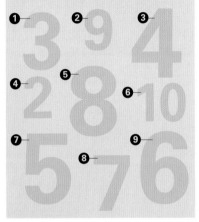

2 Hello

1 **Bonjour. Je m'appelle... [your name].**
boñjoor. juh mapell...

2 **Enchanté(e).**
oñshontay

3 **Oui, et j'ai deux fils. Et vous?**
wee, ay jay duh fees. ay voo

4 **Au revoir. A demain.**
ovwar. ah dumañ

2 Hello

You meet someone in a formal situation. Join in the conversation, replying in French according to the English prompts.

Bonjour. Je m'appelle Nicole.
1 *Answer the greeting and give your name.*

Voici mon mari, Henri.
2 *Say "Pleased to meet you".*

Vous êtes marié(e)?
3 *Say "Yes, and I have two sons. And you?"*

Nous avons trois filles.
4 *Say "Goodbye. See you tomorrow".*

3 To have or be

Fill in the blanks with the correct form of **avoir** (*to have*) or **être** (*to be*). Check you have remembered the French correctly.

1 Je _____ anglaise.

2 Nous _____ quatre enfants.

3 Elle _____ une belle-fille.

4 Vous _____ rendez-vous?

5 Il n' _____ pas fatigué.

6 Je n' _____ pas de portable.

7 Tu n' _____ pas sûr?

8 Nous _____ français.

3 To have or be

1 **suis**
swee

2 **avons**
avoñ

3 **a**
ah

4 **avez**
avay

5 **est**
ay

6 **ai**
ay

7 **es**
ay

8 **sommes**
som

4 Family

Say the French for each of the numbered family members. Check you have remembered the French correctly.

grandfather ❶ brother ❷ ❸ sister ❹ father ❺ mother
grandmother ❻ ❼ son ❽ daughter

4 Family

1 **le grand-père**
luh groñpair

2 **le frère**
luh frair

3 **la soeur**
lah sur

4 **le père**
luh pair

5 **la mère**
lah mair

6 **la grand-mère**
lah groñmair

7 **le fils**
luh fees

8 **la fille**
lah feeyuh

Count to ten
(pp.10–11).

Remind yourself how
to say "hello" and
"goodbye". (pp.8–9)

Ask "Do you have a
baguette?" (pp.14–15)

Au café
In the café

In a typical French café you can either
sit at the counter, which is cheaper,
or have waiter service at a table.
Tipping is the norm if you're happy
with the service, but a few coins will
be enough. Food is not usually served,
although you can often get bread and
croissants in the mornings.

2 Words to remember

Look at the words below and say them out
loud a few times. Cover the French with the
flap and try to remember the French for each
item. Practise the words on the picture also.

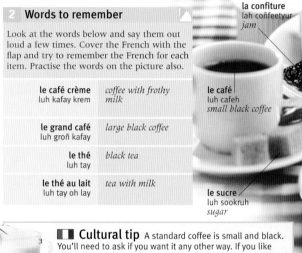

la confiture
lah coñfeetyur
jam

le café
luh cafeh
small black coffee

le sucre
luh sookruh
sugar

le café crème luh kafay krem	*coffee with frothy milk*
le grand café luh groñ kafay	*large black coffee*
le thé luh tay	*black tea*
le thé au lait luh tay oh lay	*tea with milk*

Cultural tip A standard coffee is small and black.
You'll need to ask if you want it any other way. If you like
milk in your tea, you'll need to specify cold milk ("lait froid"/
lay frwah), otherwise you are likely to get a jug of hot milk.

3 In conversation

**Bonjour. Je voudrais
un café au lait, s'il
vous plaît.**
bonjoor. juh voodray uñ
kafay oh lay, seel voo
play

*Hello. I would like a
white coffee, please.*

C'est tout madame?
say too ma-dam

Is that all madam?

**Vous avez des
croissants?**
voo zavay day krossoñ

*Do you have any
croissants?*

4 Useful phrases

Learn these phrases. Read the English under the pictures and say the phrase in French as shown on the right. Then conceal the French with the cover flap and test yourself.

le pain
luh pañ
bread

Je voudrais un grand café, s'il vous plaît.
juh voodray uñ groñ kafay, seel voo play

I'd like a large black coffee, please.

C'est tout?
say too

Is that all?

Je prends un croissant.
juh pron uñ krossoñ

I'll have a croissant.

le café au lait
luh kafay oh lay
large coffee with milk

C'est combien?
say koñbyañ

How much is that?

Oui, bien sûr.
wee, byañ syur

Yes, certainly.

Alors deux croissants. C'est combien?
alor duh krossoñ. say koñbyañ

Two croissants then. How much is that?

Quatre euros, s'il vous plaît.
katruh uroh, seel voo play

Four euros, please.

Say "I'd like".
(pp.18–19)

Say "I don't have a brother". (pp.14–15)

Ask "Do you have any croissants?"
(pp.18–19)

Au restaurant
In the restaurant

There is a variety of different types of eating place in France. In a **café** you can find a few snacks. A **brasserie** is a traditional restaurant; the service is fast and there's usually no need to book. In the more formal gastronomic restaurants, it is necessary to book and to dress smartly.

Memorize these words. Conceal the French with the cover flap and test yourself.

la carte lah kart	*menu*
la carte des vins lah kart day vañ	*wine list*
les entrées *(f)* lay zontray	*starters*
les plats *(m)* lay plah	*main courses*
les desserts *(m)* lay dessair	*desserts*
le déjeuner luh dayjunay	*lunch*
le dîner luh deenay	*dinner*
le petit-déjeuner luh puhtee dayjunay	*breakfast*

cup **7**

knife **6**

5 *spoon*   **4** *fork*

Bonjour. Je voudrais une table pour quatre.
boñjoor. juh voodray oon tabluh poor katruh

Hello. I would like a table for four.

Vous avez une réservation?
voo zavay oon raysairvasyoñ

Do you have a reservation?

Oui, au nom de Smith.
wee, oh noñ duh Smith

Yes, in the name of Smith.

4 Match and repeat

Look at the numbered items in this table setting and match them with the French words on the right. Read the French words aloud. Now, conceal the French with the cover flap and test yourself.

glass **1**

8 *saucer*

1	**le verre**	luh vair
2	**la serviette**	lah sairvyet
3	**l'assiette** *(f)*	lasyet
4	**la fourchette**	lah forshet
5	**la cuillère**	lah kweeyair
6	**le couteau**	luh kootoe
7	**la tasse**	lah tass
8	**la soucoupe**	lah sookoop

5 Useful phrases

Learn these phrases and then test yourself using the cover flap to conceal the French.

napkin **2**

What do you have for dessert?	**Qu'est ce que vous avez comme dessert?** keskuh voo zavay kom dessair
The bill, please.	**L'addition, s'il vous plait.** ladeesyoñ, seel voo play

plate **3**

D'accord. Quelle table vous préférez?
dakor. kel tabluh voo prayfayray

Fine. Which table would you like?

Près de la fenêtre, s'il vous plaît.
pray duh lah fenetruh, seel voo play

Near the window please.

Mais bien sûr. Suivez-moi.
may byañ syur. sweevay mwah

But of course. Follow me.

1 Warm up

What are "breakfast", "lunch", and "dinner" in French? (pp.20–1)

Say "I", "you" (informal), "he", "she", "we", "you" (plural/formal), "they" (masculine), "they" (feminine). (pp.14–15)

Vouloir
To want

In this section, you will learn the present tense of a verb that is essential to everyday conversation – **vouloir** (*to want*) – as well as a useful polite form, **je voudrais** (*I would like*). Remember to use this form when requesting something because **je veux** (*I want*) may sound too strong.

2 Vouloir: to want

Say the different forms of **vouloir** (*to want*) aloud. Use the cover flaps to test yourself and, when you are confident, practise the sample sentences below.

je veux juh vuh	*I want*
tu veux tew vuh	*you want (informal)*
il/elle veut eel/el vuh	*he/she wants*
nous voulons noo vooloñ	*we want*
vous voulez voo voolay	*you want (formal/plural)*
ils/elles veulent eel/el verl	*they want*
Tu veux du vin? tew vuh dew vañ	*Do you want some wine?*
Elle veut une nouvelle voiture. el vuh oon noovel vwatyur	*She wants a new car.*
Nous voulons aller en vacances. noo vooloñ zallay oñ vakons	*We want to go on holiday.*

Je veux des bonbons.
juh vuh day boñ-boñ
I want some sweets.

■■ Conversational tip To say "some", "de" ("of") combines with "le", "la", or "les" to produce "du" for the masculine, "de la" for feminine, or "des" for the plural, as in "du café", "de la confiture", and "des citrons" (lemons). If the sentence is negative, use only "de", as in "Il n'y a pas de café". In the same way, à ("to") combines with "le", "la", or "les" to produce "au" for the masculine, "à la" for the feminine, and "aux" for the plural.

3 Polite requests

There is a form of **je veux** (*I want*) used for polite requests: **je voudrais**. Practise the sentences below and then test yourself.

I'd like a beer, please.	**Je voudrais une bière, s'il vous plaît.** juh voodray oon biyair, seel voo play
I'd like a table for tonight.	**Je voudrais une table pour ce soir.** juh voodray oon tabluh poor suh swar
I'd like the menu.	**Je voudrais la carte.** juh voodray lah kart

4 Put into practice

Join in this conversation. Read the French beside the pictures on the left and then follow the English prompts to make your reply in French. Test yourself by concealing the answers with the cover flap.

Bonsoir, madame. Vous avez une réservation?
boñswar, ma-dam. Voo zavay oon raysairvasyoñ
Good evening, madam. Do you have a reservation?

Say: No, but I would like a table for three, please.

Non, mais je voudrais une table pour trois, s'il vous plaît.
noñ, may juh voodray oon tabluh poor trwah, seel voo play

Fumeur ou non-fumeur?
foomur oo noñ-foomur
Smoking or non-smoking?

Say: I'd like non-smoking, please.

Je voudrais non-fumeur, s'il vous plaît.
juh voodray noñ-foomur, seel voo play

1 Warm up

Say "I'm tired" and "I'm not sure". (pp.14–15)

Ask "Do you have croissants?" (pp.18–19)

Say "I'd like a white coffee". (pp.18–19)

Les plats
Dishes

France is famous for its cuisine and the quality of its best restaurants. It also offers a wide variety of regional dishes. Plenty of garlic and butter are a feature of many typical dishes. Although traditionally French cuisine is meat-based, many restaurants now offer a vegetarian menu.

 Cultural tip You will usually have the choice of eating a set "menu" or ordering "à la carte". With a set menu, salad is often a starter and you usually have to choose between dessert or cheese.

2 Match and repeat

Look at the numbered items and match them to the French words in the panel on the left. Test yourself using the cover flap.

1 **les légumes** *(m)*
lay laygoom

2 **le fruit**
luh froo-wee

3 **le fromage**
luh fromarj

4 **les noix** *(f)*
lay nwah

5 **la soupe**
lah soop

6 **la volaille**
lah vol-eye

7 **le poisson**
luh pwassoñ

8 **les pâtes** *(f)*
lay pat

9 **les fruits de mer** *(m)*
lay froo-wee duh mair

10 **la viande**
lah vee-ond

❶ *vegetables*

❷ *fruit*

❸ *cheese*

❺ *soup*

❻ *poultry*

❽ *pasta*

❾ *seafood*

3 Words to remember: cooking methods

Familiarize yourself with these words and then test yourself.

fried	**frit(e)**	free(t)
grilled	**grillé(e)**	greeyay
roasted	**rôti(e)**	rotee
boiled	**bouilli(e)**	booyee
steamed	**à la vapeur**	ah lah vapur
rare	**saignant(e)**	say-nyoñ(t)

Je voudrais mon steak bien cuit.
juh voodray moñ stayk byañ kwee
I'd like my steak well done.

6 Say it

What is "cassoulet"?

I'm allergic to seafood.

I'd like a beer.

4 Words to remember: drinks

Familiarize yourself with these words.

water	**l'eau** *(f)*	loe
fizzy water	**l'eau gazeuse** *(f)*	loe gazuz
still water	**l'eau plate** *(f)*	loe plat
wine	**le vin**	luh vañ
beer	**la bière**	lah biyair
fruit juice	**le jus de fruits**	luh joo duh froo-wee

4 nuts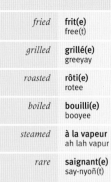

5 Useful phrases

Learn these phrases and then test yourself.

I'm a vegetarian.	**Je suis végétarien.**	juh swee vejitah-ryañ
I'm allergic to nuts.	**Je suis allergique aux noix.**	juh swee zalurzheek oh nwah
What are "escargots"?	**Qu'est que c'est les "escargots"?**	keskuh say lay zeskargoh

7 fish

10 meat
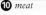

Révisez et répétez
Review and repeat

1 At table

1 **les noix**
lay nwah

2 **les fruits de mer**
lay froo-wee
duh mair

3 **la viande**
lah vee-ond

4 **le sucre**
luh sookruh

5 **le verre**
luh vair

1 At table

Name the numbered items.

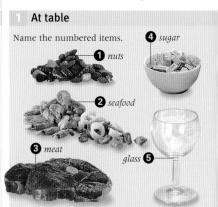

1 nuts
2 seafood
3 meat
4 sugar
glass **5**

2 This is my...

1 **C'est mon mari.**
say moñ maree

2 **Voici ma fille.**
vwasee mah feeyuh

3 **Ma table est
non-fumeur.**
mah tabluh ay noñ-
foomur

4 **Mes enfants
sont fatigués.**
may zoñfoñ soñ
fatigay

2 This is my...

Say these phrases in French.
Use **mon**, **ma**, or **mes**.

1 *This is my husband.*

2 *Here is my daughter.*

3 *My table is non-smoking.*

4 *My children are tired.*

3 I'd like...

1 **Je voudrais un
café.**
juh voodray uñ
kafay

2 **Je voudrais de la
confiture.**
juh voodray duh
lah coñfeetyur

3 **Je voudrais du
pain.**
juh voodray doo
pañ

4 **Je voudrais un
café au lait.**
juh voodray uñ
kafay oh lay

3 I'd like...

Say you'd like the following:

jam **2**   bread **3**
1 black coffee
large coffee
with milk **4**

6 *pasta*
knife 7
8 *cheese*
beer 10
9 *napkin*

Réponses
Answers
Cover with flap

1 At table

6 **les pâtes**
lay pat

7 **le couteau**
luh kootoe

8 **le fromage**
luh fromarj

9 **la serviette**
lah sairvyet

10 **la bière**
lah biyair

4 Restaurant

You arrive at a restaurant. Join in the conversation, replying in French according to the English prompts.

Bonjour madame, monsieur.
1 *Ask for a table for six.*

Fumeur ou non-fumeur?
2 *Say: non-smoking.*

Suivez-moi, s'il vous plaît.
3 *Ask for the menu.*

Et vous voulez la carte des vins?
4 *Say: No. Fizzy water, please.*

Voilà.
5 *Say: I don't have a glass.*

4 Restaurant

1 **Bonjour. Je voudrais une table pour six.**
boñjoor. juh voodray oon tabluh por sees

2 **Non-fumeur.**
noñ-foomur

3 **La carte, s'il vous plaît.**
lah kart, seel voo play

4 **Non. De l'eau gazeuse, s'il vous plaît.**
noñ. duh loe gazuz, seel voo play

5 **Je n'ai pas de verre.**
juh nay pah duh vair

1 Warm up

Say "he is" and "they are". (pp.14–15)

Say "he is not" and "they are not". (pp.14–15)

What is French for "the children"? (pp.10–11)

Les jours et les mois
Days and months

In French the days of the week (**les jours de semaine**) and months (**les mois**) do not have capital letters. The months have similar names to the English. You use **en** with months: **en avril** (*in April*), but not with days.

2 Words to remember: days

Familiarize yourself with these words and test yourself using the flap.

lundi luñdee	*Monday*	
mardi mardee	*Tuesday*	
mercredi mairkrudee	*Wednesday*	
jeudi jurdee	*Thursday*	
vendredi voñdrudee	*Friday*	
samedi samdee	*Saturday*	
dimanche deemonsh	*Sunday*	
aujourd'hui oh-joordwee	*today*	
demain dumañ	*tomorrow*	
hier eeyair	*yesterday*	

Demain, c'est lundi.
dumañ, say luñdee
Tomorrow is Monday.

3 Useful phrases: days

Learn these phrases and then test yourself using the cover flap.

La réunion n'est pas mardi. lah rayoonyoñ nay pah mardee	*The meeting isn't on Tuesday.*
Je travaille le dimanche. juh trav-eye luh deemonsh	*I work on Sundays.*

4 Words to remember: months

Familiarize yourself with these words and test yourself using the flap.

Notre anniversaire de mariage est en juillet.
notruh aneevairsair duh mareeaj ay toñ jweeyay
Our wedding anniversary is in July.

January	**janvier**	joñvyay
February	**février**	fevreeyay
March	**mars**	mars
April	**avril**	avreel
May	**mai**	may
June	**juin**	jwañ
July	**juillet**	jweeyay
August	**août**	oot
September	**septembre**	septombruh
October	**octobre**	oktobruh
November	**novembre**	novombruh
December	**décembre**	daysombruh
month	**le mois**	luh mwah
year	**l'an** *(m)*	loñ

Noël est en décembre.
nowel ay toñ daysombruh
Christmas is in December.

5 Useful phrases: months

Learn these phrases and then test yourself using the cover flap.

My children are on holiday in August.	**Mes enfants sont en vacances en août.** may zoñfoñ soñ toñ vakons oñ oot
My birthday is in June.	**Mon anniversaire est en juin.** moñ naneevairsair ay toñ jwañ

Count in French from 1 to 10. (pp.10–11)

Say "I have a reservation". (pp.20–1)

Say "The meeting is on Wednesday". (pp.28–9)

L'heure et les nombres
Time and numbers

The 12-hour clock is used in everyday speech while the 24-hour clock is employed in stations and airports, etc. While in English the minutes are first (*ten to five*), in French the hour is first: **dix heures moins cinq** (*ten minus five*).

2 Words to remember: time

Memorize how to tell the time in French.

une heure oon ur	*one o'clock*
une heure cinq oon ur sank	*five past one*
une heure et quart oon ur ay kar	*quarter past one*
une heure vingt oon ur vañ	*twenty past one*
une heure et demie oon ur ay dumee	*half past one*
deux heures moins le quart duh zur mwañ luh kar	*quarter to two*
deux heures moins dix duh zur mwañ dees	*ten to two*

3 Useful phrases

Learn these phrases and then test yourself using the cover flap.

Quelle heure est-il? kel ur ay teel	*What time is it?*
A quelle heure voulez-vous le petit déjeuner? ah kel ur voolay voo luh puhtee dayjunay	*What time do you want breakfast?*
J'ai une réservation pour douze heures. jay oon raysairvasyoñ poor dooz ur	*I have a reservation for twelve o'clock.*

4 Words to remember: higher numbers

In French when you
say 21, 31, etc. you
say: **vingt-et-un**,
trente-et-un, and so
on. After that just
put the numbers
together without
"et": **vingt-deux** (22),
quarante-cinq (45).

Seventy is **soixante-
dix** (*sixty-ten*), 75 is
soixante-quinze (*sixty-
fifteen*), and so on.
Quatre-vingt (80)
means *four-twenties*,
and 90 is **quatre-
vingt-dix** (*four-
twenties-ten*). So 82
is **quatre-vingt-deux**
and 97 is **quatre-
vingt-dix-sept**.

**Ça fait quatre-vingt-
cinq euros.**
sah fay katruh-vañ-sank
uroh
That's eighty-five euros.

5 Say it

twenty-five

sixty-eight

eighty-four

ninety-one

five to ten.

half past eleven.

What time is lunch?

eleven	**onze** onz
twelve	**douze** dooz
thirteen	**treize** trez
fourteen	**quatorze** katorz
fifteen	**quinze** kanz
sixteen	**seize** sez
seventeen	**dix-sept** deeset
eighteen	**dix-huit** deezweet
nineteen	**dix-neuf** deeznurf
twenty	**vingt** vañ
thirty	**trente** tront
forty	**quarante** karont
fifty	**cinquante** sankont
sixty	**soixante** swasont
seventy	**soixante-dix** swasont-dees
eighty	**quatre-vingt** katruh-vañ
ninety	**quatre-vingt-dix** katruh-vañ-dees
hundred	**cent** soñ
three hundred	**trois cents** trwah soñ
thousand	**mille** meel
ten thousand	**dix mille** dee meel
two hundred thousand	**deux cent mille** duh soñ meel
one million	**un million** oon meel-yoñ

1 Warm up

Say the days of the week. (pp.28–9)

Say "It's three o'clock". (pp.30–1)

What's the French for "today", "tomorrow", and "yesterday"? (pp.28–9)

Les rendez-vous
Appointments

Business in France is generally conducted more formally than in Britain or the United States; always address business contacts as **vous**. The French tend to leave the office for the lunch hour, often having a sit-down meal in a restaurant or, less commonly, at home.

2 Useful phrases

Learn these phrases and then test yourself.

Prenons rendez-vous pour demain. prunoñ ronday-voo poor dumañ	*Let's meet tomorrow.*
Avec qui? avek kee	*With whom?*
Quand êtes-vous libre? koñ et-voo leebruh	*When are you free?*
Je suis désolé(e), je suis occupé(e). juh swee dayzolay, juh swee zokupay	*I'm sorry, I'm busy.*
Pourquoi pas jeudi? poorkwah pah jurdee	*How about Thursday?*
C'est bon pour moi. say boh poor mwah	*That's good for me.*

la poignée de main
lah pwanyay duh mañ
handshake

Bienvenue.
byañvenoo
Welcome.

3 In conversation

Bonjour. J'ai rendez-vous.
boñjoor. jay ronday-voo

Hello. I have an appointment.

Avec qui?
avek kee

With whom?

Avec Monsieur Le Blanc.
avek musyuh luh bloñ

With Mr Le Blanc.

4 Put into practice

Join in this conversation. Read the French beside the pictures on the left and then follow the instructions to make your reply. Then test yourself by concealing the answers on the right with the cover flap.

	Prenons rendez-vous pour jeudi. prunoñ ronday-voo poor jurdee *Let's meet on Thursday.* Say: Sorry, I'm busy.	**Je suis désolé, je suis occupé.** juh swee dayzolay, juh swee zokupay
	Quand êtes-vous libre? koñ et-voo leebruh *When are you free?* Say: Tuesday afternoon.	**Mardi après-midi.** mardee apray meedee
	C'est bon pour moi. say boñ poor mwa *That's good for me.* Ask: What time?	**A quelle heure?** ah kel ur
	A quatre heures, si c'est bon pour vous. ah katruh ur see say boñ poor voo *At four o'clock, if that's good for you.* Say: It's good for me.	**C'est bon pour moi.** say boñ poor mwah

Très bien. A quelle heure?
tray byañ. ah kel ur

Very good. What time?

A trois heures, mais je suis un peu en retard.
ah trwah zur, may juh swee uñ puh oñ retar

At three o'clock, but I'm a little late.

Ne vous inquiétez pas. Asseyez-vous, je vous en prie.
nuh voo zañkyetay pah. assayay voo, juh voo zoñ pree

Don't worry. Sit down, please.

1 Warm up

Say "I'm sorry".
(pp.32–3)

What is the French for "I'd like an appointment"?
(pp.32–3)

How do you say "with whom?" in French?
(pp.32–3)

Au téléphone
On the telephone

In France the emergency police number is 17; ambulance 15; fire 18; and directory enquiries 12. Telephone cards (**télécartes**) can be used for public phones or private phones by tapping in a code. They are available from post offices and newsagents.

2 Match and repeat

Match the numbered items to the French in the panel on the left and test yourself.

1 **le chargeur**
luh sharjur

2 **les renseigne-ments** *(m)*
lay ronsenyumoñ

3 **le répondeur**
luh raypoñdur

4 **le téléphone**
luh telayfon

5 **le portable**
luh portabluh

6 **la télécarte**
lah telaykart

7 **les écouteurs** *(m)*
lay zaykootur

❶ charger

❹ telephone

❺ mobile

❼ headphones   phonecard ❻

3 In conversation

Allô. Pauline Du Bois à l'appareil.
aloh. pawleen doo bwah ah lap-paray

Hello. Pauline du Bois speaking.

Bonjour. Je voudrais parler à Rachid Djamal.
boñjoor. juh voodray parlay ah rasheed jahmal

Hello. I'd like to speak to Rachid Djamal.

C'est de la part de qui?
say duh lah par duh kee

Who's speaking?

4 Useful phrases

Practise these phrases. Then test yourself using the cover flap.

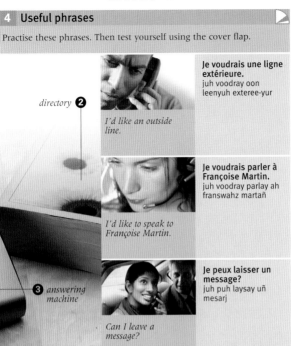

directory **2**

Je voudrais une ligne extérieure.
juh voodray oon leenyuh exteree-yur

I'd like an outside line.

Je voudrais parler à Françoise Martin.
juh voodray parlay ah franswahz martañ

I'd like to speak to Françoise Martin.

3 *answering machine*

Je peux laisser un message?
juh puh laysay uñ mesarj

Can I leave a message?

5 Say it

I'd like to speak to Mr Hachart.

Can I leave a message for Emma?

Désolé(e), je me suis trompé(e) de numéro.
dayzolay, juh muh swee trompay duh noomairoe

Sorry I have the wrong number.

Jean Leblanc de l'imprimerie Laporte.
joñ luhbloñ duh lahpreemuree laport

Jean Leblanc of Laporte Printers.

Désolée. La ligne est occupée.
dayzolay. lah leenyuh et okupay

I'm sorry. The line is busy.

Il peut me rappeller, s'il vous plaît?
eel puh muh raplay, seel voo play

Can he call me back, please?

Révisez et répétez
Review and repeat

Réponses
Answers
Cover with flap

1 Sums

1 **seize**
sez

2 **trente-neuf**
tront-nurf

3 **cinquante-trois**
sankont-trwah

4 **soixante-quatorze**
swasont-katorz

5 **quatre-vingt dix-neuf**
katruh-vañ deeznuf

6 **quarante-et-un**
karont-ay-uñ

1 Sums

Say the answers to these sums out loud in French. Then check you have remembered correctly.

1 $10 + 6 = ?$

2 $14 + 25 = ?$

3 $66 - 13 = ?$

4 $40 + 34 = ?$

5 $90 + 9 = ?$

6 $46 - 5 = ?$

3 Telephones

What are the numbered items in French?

mobile **1**

phonecard **3**

2 I want...

1 **voulez**
voolay

2 **veut**
vuh

3 **voulons**
vooloñ

4 **veux**
vuh

5 **veux**
vuh

6 **veut**
vuh

2 I want...

Fill the blanks with the correct form of **vouloir**.

1 Vous _____ un café?

2 Elle _____ aller en vacances.

3 Nous _____ une table pour trois.

4 Tu _____ une bière?

5 Je _____ une nouvelle voiture.

6 Il _____ des bonbons.

answering machine

telephone ❹ *headphones* ❺

3 Telephones

1 **le portable**
luh portabluh

2 **le répondeur**
luh raypoñdur

3 **la télécarte**
lah telaykart

4 **le téléphone**
luh telayfon

5 **les écouteurs**
lay zaykootur

4 When?

What do these sentences mean?

1 **J'ai rendez-vous lundi vingt mai.**

2 **Mon anniversaire est en septembre.**

3 **Je reviens dimanche.**

4 **Ils ne travaillent pas en août.**

4 When?

1 *I have a meeting on Monday 20th May.*

2 *My birthday is in September.*

3 *I come back on Sunday.*

4 *They don't work in August.*

5 Time

Say these times in French.

❶ ❷
❸ ❹
❺ ❻

5 Time

1 **une heure**
oon ur

2 **une heure cinq**
oon ur sank

3 **une heure vingt**
oon ur vañ

4 **une heure et demie**
oon ur ay dumee

5 **une heure et quart**
oon ur ay kar

6 **deux heures moins dix**
duh zur mwañ dees

Count to 100 in tens.
(pp.10–11, pp.30–1)

Ask "At what time?"
(pp.30–1)

Say "Half-past one".
(pp.30–1)

Au guichet
At the ticket office

In France, before getting on the train, you must validate (**composter**) your ticket by stamping it. Special orange machines are installed in every train station for this purpose. Fines are handed out to those who forget to validate their tickets. Most trains have both first and second class seats.

2 Words to remember

Learn these words and then test yourself.

la gare lah gar	*station*
le train luh trañ	*train*
la voiture lah vwatyur	*carriage*
le billet luh beeyay	*ticket*
aller-simple allay-sañpluh	*single*
aller-retour allay-rutoor	*return*
première classe prumyair klas	*first class*
en seconde oñ sugond	*second class*

le quai
luh kay
platform

le passager
luh pasahjay
passenger

La gare est pleine de monde.
lah gar ay plen duh moñd
The station is crowded.

3 In conversation

Deux billets pour Bordeaux s'il vous plaît.
duh beeyay poor bordoe seel voo play

Two tickets for Bordeaux please.

Aller-retour?
allay rutoor

Return?

Oui. Je dois réserver des places?
wee. juh dwah rayzurvay day plas

Yes. Do I need to reserve seats?

4 Useful phrases

Learn these phrases and then test yourself using the cover flap.

How much is a ticket to Lille?

C'est combien un billet pour Lille?
say koñbyañ uñ beeyay poor leel

Do you accept credit cards?

Vous acceptez les cartes de crédit?
voo zakseptay lay kart duh kredee

Do I have to change?

Je dois changer?
juh dwah shonjay

Which platform does the train leave from?

Le train part de quel quai?
luh trañ par duh kel kay

Are there discounts?

Vous faites des réductions?
voo fet day raydooksyoñ

Le train pour Poitiers est annulé.
luh trañ poor pwatyer et anulay
The train for Poitiers is cancelled.

What time does the train for Paris leave?

A quelle heure part le train pour Paris?
ah kel ur par luh trañ poor paree

5 Say it

Which platform does the train for Paris leave from?

Three tickets to Lyon, please.

🇫🇷 Cultural tip
Most train stations now have automatic ticket machines that accept credit and debit cards as well as cash.

Ce n'est pas nécessaire. Quarante euros s'il vous plaît.
suh nay pah nesaysair. karont uroh seel voo play

That's not necessary. Forty euros please.

Vous acceptez les cartes de crédit?
voo zakseptay lay kart duh kredee

Do you accept credit cards?

Bien sûr. Le train part du quai numéro cinq.
byañ syur. luh trañ par doo kay noomairoe sank

Certainly. The train leaves from platform five.

1 Warm up

How do you say "train"? (pp.38–9)

What does "Le train part de quel quai?" mean? (pp.38–9)

Ask "When are you free?" (pp.32–3)

Aller et prendre
To go and to take

Aller (*to go*) and **prendre** (*to take*) are essential verbs in French. You can also use **prendre** to say *I'll have* (**je prends**) when you talk about food and drink. Note that the present tense in French includes the sense of a continuous action – for example, **je vais** means both *I go* and *I am going*.

2 Aller: to go

Say the different forms of **aller** (*to go*) aloud. Use the flaps to test yourself and, when you are confident, practise the sample sentences below.

je vais juh vay	*I go*
tu vas tew vah	*you go (informal singular)*
il/elle va eel/el vah	*he/she goes*
nous allons noo zalloñ	*we go*
vous allez voo zallay	*you go (formal singular or plural)*
ils/elles vont eel/el voñ	*they go*
Où allez-vous? oo allay voo	*Where are you going?*
Je vais à Paris. juh vay zah paree	*I'm going to Paris.*
Nous allons à l'école en train. noo zalloñ ah laykol oñ trañ	*We go to school by train.*

Je vais à la Tour Eiffel.
juh vay zah lah toor eefel
I'm going to the Eiffel Tower.

🔲 **Cultural tip** The TGV ("train à grande vitesse") is a fast train that can get you from Paris to the south of France in about three hours. Generally you will need to reserve a seat and can still choose smoking or non-smoking seats. TER ("trains express régionaux") is another type of fast train. These trains are cheaper than the TGV. You can buy a ticket on the day of travel and get on without a reservation.

3 Prendre: to take

Say the different forms of **prendre** (*to take*) aloud. Use the flaps to cover the French and test yourself. When you are confident, practise the sample sentences below.

Je prends le métro tous les jours.
juh proñ luh metroe too lay joor
I take the metro every day.

I take	**je prends** juh proñ	
you take (informal singular)	**tu prends** tew proñ	
he/she takes	**il/elle prend** eel/el proñ	
we take	**nous prenons** noo prunoñ	
you take (formal singular or plural)	**vous prenez** voo prunay	
they take	**ils/elles prennent** eel/el pren	

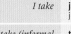

I don't want to take a taxi.	**Je ne veux pas prendre un taxi.** juh nuh vuh pah proñdruh uñ taksee
Take the first on the left.	**Prenez la première à gauche.** prunay lah prumyair ah gaush
He'll have the beef bourguignon.	**Il prend le bœuf bourguignon.** eel proñ luh buf boorgheenyoñ

4 Put into practice

Cover the text on the right and complete the dialogue in French.

Où allez-vous? oo allay voo *Where are you going?*	**Je vais au Louvre.** juh vay zoh loovruh
Say: *I'm going to the Louvre.*	

Vous voulez prendre le métro? voo voolay proñdruh luh metroe *Do you want to take the metro?*	**Non, je veux aller en bus.** noñ juh vuh allay oñ boos
Say: *No, I want to go by bus.*	

1 Warm up

Say "I'd like to go to the station". (pp.40–1)

Ask "Where are you going?" (pp.40–1)

Say "fruit" and "cheese". (pp.24–5)

Taxi, bus, et métro
Taxi, bus, and metro

With buses, as with trains, you need to validate your ticket in a machine at the time of travel. For the metro, there's a standard fare and you can also buy a **carnet**, a book of 10 tickets. It's unusual to flag down a taxi in the street. You need to find one of the many taxi ranks and wait there.

2 Words to remember

Familiarize yourself with these words.

le bus luh boos	*bus*
le car luh kar	*coach*
la gare routière lah gar rootyair	*bus station*
l'arrêt de bus *(m)* laray duh boos	*bus stop*
le tarif luh tareef	*fare*
le taxi luh taksee	*taxi*
la rangée de taxis lah roñjay duh taksee	*taxi rank*
la station de métro lah stasyoñ duh metroe	*metro station*

Le bus numéro 4 s'arrête ici?
luh boos noomairoe katruh saret eesee
Does the number 4 bus stop here?

3 In conversation: taxi

Le marché aux fromages, s'il vous plaît.
luh marshayoe fromarj, seel voo play

The cheese market, please.

Oui, sans problème, monsieur.
wee. soñ problem musyuh

Yes, no problem, sir.

Vous pouvez me déposer ici, s'il vous plaît?
voo poovay muh dayposay eesee, seel voo play

Can you drop me here, please?

4 Useful phrases

Learn these phrases and then test yourself using the cover flap.

I want a taxi to the Arc de Triomphe.	**Je veux un taxi pour l'Arc de Triomphe.** juh vuh uh taksee poor lark duh treeoñf
When is the next bus to the station?	**Quand est le prochain bus pour la gare?** koñ ay luh proshen boos poor lah gar
How do you get to the museum?	**Pour aller au musée?** poor allay oh moozay
How long is the journey?	**Le trajet dure combien de temps?** luh trajay dyur koñbyañ duh toñ
Please wait for me.	**Attendez-moi s'il vous plaît.** atonday-mwah seel voo play

---

🇫🇷 Cultural tip Métro lines ("lignes") in Paris are known by the names of the first and last stations on the line. Follow the signs to the relevant end station – for example, direction Porte d'Orléans. Look out for the beautiful art deco "Métropolitain" signs retained in some stations.

6 Say it

Do you go near the train station?

The fruit market, please.

When's the next coach to Calais?

5 In conversation: bus

Vous allez près du musée? vooz allay pray doo moozay

Do you go near the museum?

Oui. Ça fait quatre-vingt centimes. wee. sah fay katruh vañ sonteem

Yes. That's 80 cents.

Dites-moi quand on arrive, s'il vous plaît. deet mwah koñ toñ areev, seel voo play

Tell me when we arrive, please.

1 Warm up

How do you say "I have..."? (pp.14–15)

Say "my father", "my sister", and "my parents". (pp.16–17)

Say "I'm going to Paris". (pp.40–1)

En route
On the road

Be sure to familiarize yourself with the French rules of the road before driving in France. French **autoroutes** (*motorways*) are fast but expensive. They are toll (**péage**) roads in which you usually take a ticket as you join the motorway and pay according to the distance travelled as you leave it.

2 Match and repeat

Match the numbered items to the list on the left, then test yourself.

1 **le coffre**
luh kofrue

2 **le pare-brise**
luh parbreez

3 **le capot**
luh kapoh

4 **le pneu**
luh pnuh

5 **la roue**
lah roo

6 **la portière**
lah portyair

7 **le pare-chocs**
luh parshok

8 **les phares**
lay far

Cultural tip Self-service petrol stations can be unmanned. In this case, you usually have to specify how many litres you want and pay by card *before* filling up.

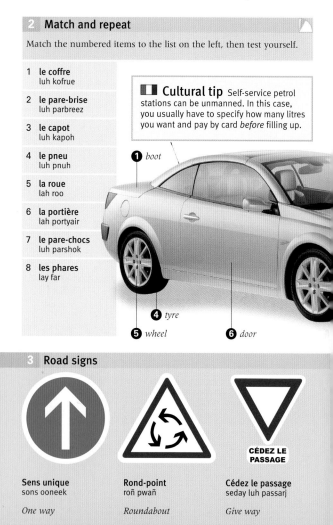

❶ *boot*
❹ *tyre*
❺ *wheel*
❻ *door*

3 Road signs

Sens unique
sons ooneek

One way

Rond-point
roñ pwañ

Roundabout

Cédez le passage
CÉDEZ LE PASSAGE
seday luh passarj

Give way

4 Useful phrases

Learn these phrases and then test yourself using the cover flap.

My indicator doesn't work.	**Mon clignotant ne marche pas.** moñ kleenyoe-toñ nuh marsh pah	
Fill it up, please.	**Le plein, s'il vous plaît.** luh plañ, seel voo play	

5 Words to remember

Familiarize yourself with these words then test yourself using the flap.

6 Say it

My gearbox doesn't work.

I have a flat tyre.

car	**la voiture** lah vwatyur
petrol	**l'essence** *(f)* laysans
diesel	**le gazole** luh gazol
oil	**l'huile** *(f)* lweel
engine	**le moteur** luh motur
gearbox	**la boîte de vitesses** lah bwat duh veetess
flat tyre	**le pneu crevé** luh pnuh kruvay
exhaust	**le pot d'échappement** luh poe dayshapmoñ
driving licence	**le permis de conduire** luh pairmee duh kondweer

2 *windscreen*

3 *bonnet*

MEGANE

7 *bumper*   *headlights* **8**

Passage protégé passarj protayjay

Priority road

Sens interdit sons añtairdee

No entry

Défense de stationner dayfoñs duh stahseeonay

No parking

Révisez et répétez
Review and repeat

1 Transport

1 **le bus**
luh boos

2 **le taxi**
luh taksee

3 **la voiture**
lah vwatyur

4 **le train**
luh trañ

5 **le vélo**
luh vayloe

6 **le métro**
luh metroe

1 Transport

Name these forms of transport in French.

bus **1**

2 tax

4 train

2 Go and take

1 **allons**
alloñ

2 **vais**
vay

3 **prend**
proñ

4 **allez**
allay

5 **prenez**
prunay

6 **prends**
proñ

2 Go and take

Use the correct form of the verb in brackets.

1 Nous _____ à la Tour Eiffel. (aller)

2 Je _____ à la gare. (aller)

3 Elle _____ rendez-vous lundi. (prendre)

4 Où _____ -vous? (aller)

5 Que _____ -vous? (prendre)

6 Je _____ le bœuf. (prendre)

3 car

5 bicycle

6 metro

METROPOLITAIN

3 Vous or tu?

Use the correct
form of you.

1 *You are in a café.
Ask "Do you have
croissants?"*

2 *You are with a
friend. Ask "Do
you want a beer?"*

3 *A business woman
approaches you at
your company
reception. Ask
"Do you have an
appointment?"*

4 *You are on the
bus. Ask "Do you
go near the
station?"*

5 *Ask your mother
where she's going
tomorrow.*

6 *Ask your client
"Are you free on
Wednesday?"*

3 Vous or tu?

1 **Vous avez des
croissants?**
voo zavay day
krossoñ

2 **Tu veux une
bière?**
tew vuh oon biyair

3 **Vous avez
rendez-vous?**
voo zavay roñday
voo

4 **Vous allez près
de la gare?**
voo zallay pray
duh lah gar

5 **Où vas-tu
demain?**
oo vah-tew dumañ

6 **Vous êtes libre
mercredi?**
voo zet leebruh
mairkrudee

4 Tickets

You're buying tickets at a train station.
Follow the conversation, replying in French
following the numbered English prompts.

Je peux vous aider?
1 *I'd like two tickets to Lille.*

Aller-simple ou aller-retour?
2 *Return, please.*

Voilà. Cinquante euros, s'il vous plaît.
3 *What time does the train leave?*

A treize heures dix.
4 *What platform
does the train
leave from?*

**Quai numéro
sept.**
5 *Thank you.
Goodbye.*

4 Tickets

1 **Je voudrais deux
billets pour Lille.**
juh voodray duh
beeyay poor leel

2 **Aller-retour, s'il
vous plaît.**
allay rutoor, seel
voo play

3 **A quelle heure
part le train?**
ah kel ur par luh
trañ

4 **Le train part de
quel quai?**
luh trañ par duh
kel kay

5 **Merci. Au revoir.**
mairsee. ovwar

1 Warm up

Ask "How do you get to the musuem?"
(pp.42–3)

Say "I want to take the metro" and "I don't want to take a taxi".
(pp.40–1)

En ville
About town

Most French towns still have a market day and a thriving community of small shops. Even small villages usually have a mayor and a town hall. There may be parking restrictions in the town centre. Look out for signs for **parcmètres** (*pay and display*) and **défense de stationner** (*parking forbidden*).

2 Match and repeat

Match the numbered locations to the words in the panel.

1 **la mairie**
  lah mayree

2 **le pont**
  luh poñ

3 **le centre ville**
  luh sontruh veel

4 **l'église** *(f)*
  legleez

5 **le parking**
  luh parking

6 **la place**
  lah plas

7 **la galerie d'art**
  lah galree dar

8 **le musée**
  luh moozay

church ❹

town centre ❸

❶ *town hall*

❷ *bridge*

❼ *art gallery*

3 Words to remember

Familiarize yourself with these words and test yourself using the cover flap.

la station service la stasyoñ servees	*petrol station*
le syndicat d'initiative luh sañdeekar deeneesyateev	*tourist information*
le garage luh gararj	*car repair shop*
la piscine municipale lah piseen mooneeseepal	*public swimming pool*

4 Useful phrases

Learn these phrases and then test yourself using the cover flap.

	Is there an art gallery in town?	**Il y a une galerie d'art en ville?** eelyah oon galree dar oñ veel
	Is it far from here?	**C'est loin d'ici?** say lwañ deesee
	There is a swimming pool near the bridge.	**Il y a une piscine près du pont.** eelyah oon piseen pray doo poñ
	There isn't a library.	**Il n'y a pas de bibliothèque.** eenyah pah duh bib-lee-yotek

La cathédrale est au centre-ville
lah kataydral et oh sontruh veel
The cathedral is in the town centre.

5 Put into practice

Join in this conversation. Read the French on the left and follow the instructions to make your reply. Then test yourself by concealing the answers with the cover flap.

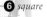
5 *car park*

6 *square*

Je peux vous aider? juh puh voo zeday *Can I help you?* *Ask: Is there a library in town?*	**Il y a une bibliothèque en ville?** eelyah oon bib-lee-yotek oñ veel
Non, mais il ya un musée. noñ may eelyah uñ moozay *No, but there's a museum.* *Ask: How do I get to the museum?*	**Pour aller au musée?** poor allay oh moozay
C'est là-bas. say lah bah *It's over there.* *Say: Thank you very much.*	**Merci beaucoup.** mairsee bohkoo

8 *museum*

1 Warm up

How do you say "near to the station"? (pp.42–3)

Say "Take the first on the left". (pp.40–1)

Ask "Where are you going?" (pp.40–1)

Les directions
Finding your way

To help you find your way, you'll often find a **plan de la ville** (*town plan*) situated in the town, usually near the town hall or tourist office. In the older parts of French towns there are often narrow streets, in which you will usually find a one-way system in operation. Parking is usually restricted.

2 Useful phrases

Learn these phrases and then test yourself.

tournez à gauche/droite toornay ah gaush/dwrat	*turn left/right*
sur la gauche/droite sewr lah gaush/dwrat	*on the right/left*
tout droit too dwrah	*straight on*
Pour aller à la piscine? poor allay ah lah piseen	*How do I get to the swimming pool?*
la première à gauche lah prumyair ah gaush	*first on the left*
la deuxième à droite lah duzyem ah dwrat	*second on the right*

le marché couvert
luh marshay coovair
indoor market

la zone piétonne
lah zohn peeayton
pedestrian zone

Tournez à gauche à la grande place
toornay ah gaush ah lah groñd plas
Turn left at the main square.

3 In conversation

Il y a un bon restaurant en ville?
eelyah uh boñ restoroñ oñ veel

Is there a good restaurant in town?

Oui, près de la gare.
wee, pray duh lah gar

Yes, near the station.

Pour aller à la gare?
poor allay ah lah gar

How do I get to the station?

4 Words to remember

Familiarize yourself with these words and test yourself using the flap.

Je me suis perdue.
juh muh swee pairdoo
I'm lost.

traffic lights	**les feux** lay fuh	
corner	**le coin** luh kwañ	
street/road	**la rue** lah roo	
main road	**la rue principale** lah roo prañseepal	
at the end	**au bout** oh boo	
map	**la carte** lah kart	
cross over	**traversez** travairsay	
opposite	**en face de** oñ fass duh	

le monument
luh moonyumoñ
monument

le plan de la ville
luh plañ duh lah veel
town plan

5 Say it

Turn right at the end of the street.

It's opposite the town hall.

It's ten minutes by bus.

Tournez à gauche aux feux et puis tout droit.
toornay ah gaush oh fuh ay pwee too dwrah

Turn left at the traffic lights and then straight on.

C'est loin?
say lwañ

Is it far?

Non, c'est cinq minutes à pied.
noñ, say sank minoot ah pyay

No, it's five minutes on foot.

1 Warm up

Say the days of the week in French. (pp.28–9)

How do you say "at six o'clock"? (pp.30–1)

Ask "What time is it?" (pp.30–1)

Le tourisme
Sightseeing

Most national museums close on Tuesdays and public holidays. Although shops are normally closed on Sundays, in tourist areas many will remain open all weekend. It is not unusual, particularly in rural areas, for shops and public buildings to close at lunch time.

2 Words to remember

Familiarize yourself with these words and test yourself using the flap.

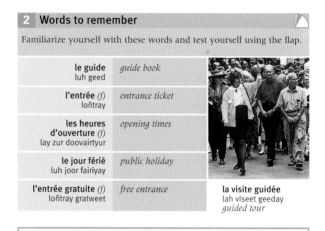

le guide luh geed	*guide book*
l'entrée (f) loñtray	*entrance ticket*
les heures d'ouverture (f) lay zur doovairtyur	*opening times*
le jour férié luh joor fairiyay	*public holiday*
l'entrée gratuite (f) loñtray gratweet	*free entrance*

la visite guidée
lah viseet geeday
guided tour

> **■ Cultural tip** The majority of public buildings and private offices close for public holidays. Many public and private offices are closed in August. If a public holiday falls on a Thursday, the French will often "faire le pont" (do the bridge) – in other words, take Friday off as well to make a long weekend.

3 In conversation

Vous ouvrez cet après-midi?
voo zoovray set apray-meedee

Do you open this afternoon?

Oui, mais nous fermons à quatre heures.
wee, may noo fairmoñ ah katruh

Yes, but we close at four o'clock.

Vous avez un accès pour les fauteuils roulants?
voo zavay uñ aksay poor lay fohtuhee roolañ

Do you have wheelchair access?

4 Useful phrases

Learn these phrases and then test yourself using the cover flap.

| | What time do you open/close? | **Vous ouvrez/fermez à quelle heure?** voo zoovray/fairmay ah kel ur |

| | Where are the toilets? | **Où sont les toilettes?** oo soñ lay twalet |

| | Is there wheelchair access? | **Il y a un accès pour les fauteuils roulants?** eelyah uñ aksay poor lay fohtuhee roolañ |

5 Put into practice

Cover the text on the right and complete the dialogue in French.

Désolé. Le musée est fermé.
dezolay. luh moozay ay fairmay
Sorry. The museum is closed.

Ask: Do you open on Tuesdays?

Vous ouvrez le mardi?
voo zoovray luh mardee

Oui, mais nous fermons tôt.
wee, may noo fairmoñ toe
Yes, but we close early.

Ask: At what time?

A quelle heure?
ah kel ur

Oui, il y a un ascenseur là-bas.
wee, eelyah uñ asoñsur lah-bah

Yes, there's a lift over there.

Merci, je voudrais quatre entrées.
mairsee, juh voodray katruh oñtray

Thank you, I'd like four entrance tickets.

Voilà, et le guide est gratuit.
vwalah, ay luh geed ay gratwee

Here you are, and the guidebook is free.

1 Warm up

Say "You're on time". (pp.14–15)

What's the French for "ticket"? (pp.38–9)

Say "I am going to New York". (pp.40–1)

A l'aéroport
At the airport

Although the airport environment is largely universal, it is sometimes useful to be able to ask your way around the terminal in French. It's a good idea to make sure you have a few one-euro coins when you arrive at the airport; you may need to pay for a baggage trolley.

2 Words to remember

Familiarize yourself with these words and test yourself using the flap.

l'enregistrement *(m)* loñrejeestrumoñ	*check-in*
le départ luh depar	*departures*
l'arrivée *(f)* lareevay	*arrivals*
la douane lah doo-an	*customs*
le contrôle des passeports luh kontrol day passpor	*passport control*
le terminal luh termee-nal	*terminal*
la porte d'embarquement lah port doñbarkumoñ	*gate*
le numéro de vol luh noomairoe duh vol	*flight number*

Quelle est la porte d'embarquement pour le vol numéro vingt-trois?
kel ay lah port doñbarkumoñ poor luh vol numairoh vañ-trwah
What gate does flight 23 leave from?

3 Useful phrases

Learn these phrases and then test yourself using the cover flap.

Le vol pour Nice est à l'heure? luh vol poor nees et ah lur	*Is the flight for Nice on time?*
Je ne trouve pas mes bagages. juh nuh troov pah may bagarj	*I can't find my baggage.*
Le vol pour Londres est retardé. luh vol poor londruh ay retarday	*The flight to London is delayed.*

4 Put into practice

Join in this conversation. Read the French on the left and follow the instructions to make your reply. Then test yourself by concealing the answers with the cover flap.

Bonsoir, monsieur. Je peux vous aider?
boñswar, musyuh. juh puh voo zayday
Good evening, sir. Can I help you?

Ask: Is the flight to Paris on time?

Le vol pour Paris est à l'heure?
luh vol poor paree et ah lur

Oui, monsieur
wee musyuh
Yes, sir.

Ask: What gate does it leave from?

Quelle est la porte d'embarquement?
kel ay lah port doñbarkumoñ

5 Match and repeat

Match the numbered items to the French words in the panel.

boarding pass ❶

baggage check-in ❷

ticket ❸

passport ❹

❺ suitcase   ❻ hand luggage

❼ trolley

1 **la carte d'embarquement**
lah kart doñbarkumoñ

2 **l'enregistrement des bagages** *(m)*
loñrejeestrumoñ day bagarj

3 **le billet**
luh beeyay

4 **le passeport**
luh passpor

5 **la valise**
lah valeez

6 **le bagage à main**
luh bagarj ah mañ

7 **le chariot**
luh shareeyoh

Réponses
Answers
Cover with flap

Révisez et répétez
Review and repeat

1 Places

1 **le musée**
luh moozay

2 **la mairie**
lah mayree

3 **le pont**
luh poñ

4 **la galerie d'art**
lah galree dar

5 **le parking**
luh parking

6 **la cathédrale**
lah kataydral

7 **la place**
lah plas

1 Places

Name the numbered places in French.

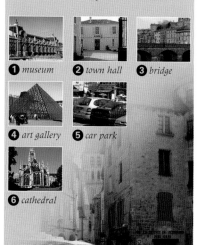

❶ *museum*   ❷ *town hall*   ❸ *bridge*

❹ *art gallery*   ❺ *car park*

❻ *cathedral*

❼ *square*

2 Car parts

1 **le pare-brise**
luh parbreez

2 **le clignotant**
luh kleenyoe-toñ

3 **le capot**
luh kapoh

4 **le pneu**
luh pnuh

5 **la portière**
lah portyair

6 **le pare-chocs**
luh parshok

2 Car parts

Name these car parts
in French.

windscreen ❶

❹ *tyre*   ❺ *door*

3 Questions

Ask the questions that match these answers.

1 **Le car part à huit heures.**
luh kar par ah weet ur

2 **Le café, c'est deux euros cinquante.**
luh kafay, say duh zuroh sankont

3 **Non, je ne veux pas de vin.**
noñ. juh nuh vuh pah duh vañ

4 **Le train part du quai cinq.**
luh trañ par doo kay sank

5 **Nous allons à Paris.**
noo zalloñ ah paree

6 **Non, c'est cinq minutes à pied.**
noñ, say sank minoot ah pyay

3 Questions

1 **Le car part à quelle heure?**
luh kar par ah kel ur

2 **C'est combien le café?**
say koñbyañ luh kafay

3 **Vous voulez du vin?**
voo voolay doo vañ

4 **Le train part de quel quai?**
luh trañ par duh kel kay

5 **Où allez-vous?**
oo allay voo

6 **C'est loin?**
say lwañ

4 Verbs

Choose the correct words to fill the gaps.

1 Je ___ anglais.

2 Nous ___ le bus.

3 Elle ___ à Paris.

4 Il ___ trois filles.

5 Tu ___ un thé?

6 Combien d'enfants ___ -vous?

7 Je ___ rendez-vous pour mardi.

8 Où ___ les toilettes?

2 *indicator*

3 *bonnet*

MEGANE

6 *bumper*

4 Verbs

1 **suis**
swee

2 **prenons**
prunoñ

3 **va**
vah

4 **a**
ah

5 **veux**
vuh

6 **avez**
avay

7 **prends**
proñ

8 **sont**
soñ

1 Warm up

How do you ask in French "Do you accept credit cards?" (pp.38–9)

Ask "How much is that?" (pp.18–19)

Ask "Do you have children?" (pp.12–13)

Réserver les chambres
Booking a room

There are different types of accommodation: **l'hôtel**, categorized from one to five stars; **la pension**, a small family-run hotel; and **les chambres d'hôte** (like bed and breakfast) which are often situated in beautiful old properties.

2 Useful phrases

Practise these phrases and then test yourself by concealing the French on the left with the cover flap.

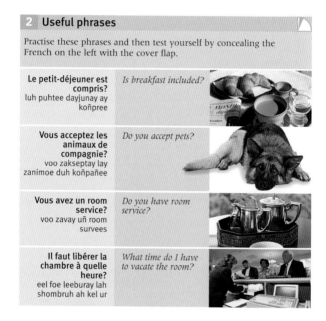

Le petit-déjeuner est compris? luh puhtee dayjunay ay koñpree	*Is breakfast included?*
Vous acceptez les animaux de compagnie? voo zakseptay lay zanimoe duh koñpañee	*Do you accept pets?*
Vous avez un room service? voo zavay uñ room survees	*Do you have room service?*
Il faut libérer la chambre à quelle heure? eel foe leeburay lah shombruh ah kel ur	*What time do I have to vacate the room?*

3 In conversation

Vous avez des chambres libres?
voo zavay day shombruh leebruh

Do you have any vacancies?

Oui, une chambre double.
wee, oon shombruh doobluh

Yes, a double room.

Vous avez un lit d'enfant?
voo zavay uñ lee doñfoñ

Do you have a cot?

4 Words to remember

Familiarize yourself with these words and test yourself by concealing the French on the right with the cover flap.

La chambre donne sur le jardin?
lah shombruh don syur luh jardañ
Does the room have a view over the garden?

room	**la chambre** lah shombruh
single room	**la chambre simple** lah shombruh sampluh
double room	**la chambre double** lah shombruh doobluh
twin room	**la chambre twin** lah shombruh twin
bathroom	**la salle de bains** lah sal duh bañ
shower	**la douche** lah doosh
breakfast	**le petit-déjeuner** luh puhtee dayjunay
key	**la clé** lah klay
balcony	**le balcon** luh balkoñ
air-conditioning	**la climatisation** lah kleematee-zasyoñ

5 Say it

Do you have a single room?

Does the room have a balcony?

Cultural tip "Chambres d'hôte" are usually the only type of accommodation to include breakfast in the price of the room. In other types of hotel you will usually be charged extra. Many two- or three-star hotels belong to the Logis de France association, which guarantees standards of accommodation and service.

Pas de problème. Combien de nuits?
pah duh prob-lem. koñbyañ duh nwee

No problem. How many nights?

Pour trois nuits.
poor trwah nwee

For three nights.

Très bien. Voici la clé.
tray byañ. vwasee lah klay

Very good. Here's the key.

1 Warm up

How do you say "is there...?" and "there isn't..."? (pp.48–9)

What does "Je peux vous aider?" mean? (pp.48–9)

A l'hôtel
In the hotel

Although the larger hotels almost always have bathrooms en suite, there are still some **pensions** and **chambres d'hôte** with shared facilities. This can also be the case in some economy hotels, where a whole family can stay the night for less than the price of a tank of petrol.

2 Match and repeat

Match the numbered items in this hotel bedroom with the French text in the panel and test yourself using the cover flap.

1 **la table de chevet**
lah tabluh duh shuvay

2 **la lampe**
lah lomp

3 **la stéréo**
lah stairayoe

4 **les rideaux** *(m)*
lay reedoe

5 **le canapé**
luh kanapay

6 **l'oreiller** *(m)*
lorayay

7 **le coussin**
luh koosañ

8 **le lit**
luh lee

9 **le dessus de lit**
luh dusoo duh lee

10 **la couverture**
lah coovurtyur

❶ *bedside table*

❷ *lamp*

❸ *music system*

❹ *curtains*

sofa ❺

❽ *bed*

blanket ❿

❻ *pillow*

❼ *cushion*

❾ *bedspread*

🔵 **Cultural tip** When you arrive in your room, you will usually see a long sausage-shaped pillow on the bed called "le traversin" – nowadays a largely decorative item. These are hard and not very comfortable. However, you can usually find square, softer pillows ("les oreillers") in the cupboard. Do not hesitate to ask if you can't find any.

3 Useful phrases

Familiarize yourself with these phrases and then test yourself.

	The room is too cold/hot.	**La chambre est trop froide/chaude.** lah shombruh ay troe fwrard/shohd
	There are no towels.	**Il n'y a pas de serviettes.** eenyah pah duh survyet
	I need some soap.	**J'ai besoin de savon.** jay buzwañ duh savoñ
	The shower doesn't work very well.	**La douche ne marche pas très bien.** lah doosh nuh marsh pah tray byañ
	The lift has broken down.	**L'ascenseur est en panne.** lasohsur ay toñ pan

4 Put into practice

Cover the text on the right and complete the dialogue in French.

Je peux vous aider?
juh puh voo zayday
Can I help you?

Say: I need some pillows.

J'ai besoin d'oreillers.
jay buzwañ dorayay

La femme de chambre va les apporter.
la fam duh shambruh vah lay zaportay
The maid will bring some.

Say: And the television doesn't work.

Et la télévision ne marche pas.
ay lah telayveesyoñ nuh marsh pah

Warm up

Ask "Can I?" (pp.34–5)

What is French for "the shower"? (pp.60–1)

Say "I need some towels". (pp.60–1)

Au camping
At the campsite

Camping is popular in France and there are many well-organized campsites. These are rated by a star system. Most towns have **un camping municipal** (*public campsite*), and there are also many private sites. Campfires are usually forbidden, but you can often hire a barbecue.

Useful phrases

Familiarize yourself with these phrases and then test yourself using the cover flap.

Je peux louer un vélo? juh puh looway uñ vayloe	*Can I rent a bicycle?*
C'est de l'eau potable? say duh loe potabluh	*Is this drinking water?*
Les feux de camp sont permis? lay fuh duh koñ soñ pairmee	*Are campfires allowed?*
Les radios sont interdites. lay radyo soñ añtairdeet	*Radios are forbidden.*

Le camping est tranquille
luh komping ay troñkeel
The campsite is quiet.

le bureau du camping
luh buroh doo komping
campsite office

la poubelle
lah poobel
litter bin

le double toit
luh doobluh twah
fly sheet

In conversation

J'ai besoin d'un emplacement pour trois nuits.
jay buzwañ d'uñ oñplasmoñ poor trwah nwee

I need a pitch for three nights.

Il y en a un près de la piscine.
eelyon ah uñ pray duh lah piseen

There's one near the swimming pool.

C'est combien pour une caravane?
say koñbyañ poor oon karavan

How much is it for a caravan?

4 **Words to remember**

Familiarize yourself with these words and test yourself using the flap.

5 **Say it**

I need a pitch for four nights.

Can I rent a tent?

Where's the electrical hook-up?

tent	**la tente**	lah tont
caravan	**la caravane**	lah karavan
camper van	**le camping-car**	luh komping-car
campsite	**le camping**	luh komping
pitch	**l'emplacement** *(m)*	loñplasmoñ
campfire	**le feu de camp**	luh fuh duh koñ
drinking water	**l'eau potable** *(f)*	loe potabluh
rubbish	**les détritus** *(m)*	lay daytreetoo
showers	**les douches** *(f)*	lay doosh
camping gas	**le camping-gaz**	luh komping-gaz
sleeping bag	**le sac de couchage**	luh sak duh koosharj
air mattress	**le matelas pneumatique**	luh mataylah nyumateek
ground sheet	**le tapis de sol**	luh tapee duh sol

les toilettes *(f)*
lay twalet
toilets

le branchement électrique
luh bronshmoñ aylektreek
electrical hook-up

la corde
lah kord
guy rope

le piquet
luh peekay
tent peg

Cinquante euros, avec une nuit d'avance.
sankoñt uroh, avek oon nwee davons

Fifty euros, one night in advance.

Je peux louer un barbecue?
juh puh looway uñ barbekyoo

Can I rent a barbecue?

Oui, mais vous devez verser des arrhes.
wee, may voo duvay vairsay day zar

Yes, but you must pay a deposit.

Révisez et répétez
Review and repeat

1 Adjectives

1 **chaude**
shohd

2 **mou**
moo

3 **bon**
boñ

4 **petite**
puhteet

5 **tranquille**
troñkeel

1 Adjectives

Put the adjective in brackets into French,
using the correct masculine or feminine form.

1 La chambre est trop ____ . (hot)

2 Je voudrais un oreiller plus ____ . (soft)

3 Le café est ____ . (good)

4 Cette salle de bains est trop ____ . (small)

5 Vous avez une chambre plus ____ ? (quiet)

2 Campsite

1 **le branchement
électrique**
luh bronshmoñ
aylektreek

2 **la tente**
lah tont

3 **la poubelle**
lah poobel

4 **la corde**
lah kord

5 **les toilettes**
lay twalet

6 **la caravane**
lah karavan

2 Campsite

Name these items you might find
in a campsite.

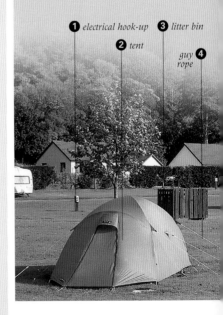

❶ *electrical hook-up*   ❸ *litter bin*

❷ *tent*

guy ❹
rope

3 At the hotel

You are booking a room in a hotel. Follow the conversation, replying in French following the English prompts.

Je peux vous aider?
1 *Do you have any vacancies?*

Oui, une chambre double.
2 *Do you accept pets?*

Oui. C'est pour combien de nuits?
3 *Three nights.*

Ça fait deux cent quarante euros.
4 *Is breakfast included?*

Bien sûr, voici la clé.
5 *Thank you very much.*

3 At the hotel

1 **Vous avez des chambres libres?**
voo zavay day shombruh leebruh

2 **Vous acceptez les animaux de compagnie?**
voo zakseptay lay zanimoe duh koñpañee

3 **Trois nuits.**
trwah nwee

4 **Le petit-déjeuner est compris?**
luh puhtee dayjuhnay ay koñpree

5 **Merci beaucoup.**
mairsee bohkoo

---

5 toilets

6 caravan

4 Negatives

Make these sentences negative using the verb in brackets.

1 Je _____ d'enfants. (avoir)

2 Elle _____ à Paris demain. (aller)

3 Il _____ de vin. (vouloir)

4 Je _____ le train pour Nice. (prendre)

5 Le café _____ chaud. (être)

4 Negatives

1 **n'ai pas**
nay pah

2 **ne va pas**
nuh vah pah

3 **ne veut pas**
nuh vuh pah

4 **ne prends pas**
nuh proñ pah

5 **n'est pas**
nay pah

Les magasins
Shops

In town centres, shops (**magasins**) are often traditional, specialist outlets. But you can also find big supermarkets and shopping malls on the outskirts of major towns. Local markets selling fresh, local produce can be found everywhere. You can find out the market day at the tourist office.

2 Match and repeat

Match the numbered shops below and right to the French in the panel. Then test yourself using the cover flap.

1 **la boulangerie**
  lah booloñjuree

2 **la pâtisserie**
  lah pateesree

3 **le tabac**
  luh tabah

4 **la boucherie**
  lah boosheree

5 **la charcuterie**
  lah sharkooterie

6 **la librairie**
  lah leebrairee

7 **la poissonnerie**
  lah pwasoñree

8 **l'épicerie** *(m)*
  laypeesree

9 **la banque**
  lah boñk

❶ *baker*

❷ *cake shop*

❹ *butcher*

❺ *delicatessen*

❼ *fishmonger*

❽ *grocer*

Cultural tip As well as supplying medicines and health products, a French pharmacy ("pharmacie") will sell expensive perfume and cosmetics but not generally an everyday bar of soap or a tube of toothpaste. The latter are found at the supermarket or general store. The "tabac" (tobacconist) is the place for newspapers and stamps, but also often incorporates a café and bar.

3 Words to remember

Familiarize yourself with these words and test yourself using the flap.

Où est la fleuriste?
oo ay lah flureest
Where is the florist?

hardware shop	**la quincaillerie**	lah kañkayeree
antique shop	**l'antiquaire** *(m)*	lañteekair
hairdresser	**le coiffeur**	luh kwafur
jeweller	**la bijouterie**	lah bee-jooteree
post office	**la poste**	lah post
shoemaker	**la cordonnerie**	lah kordoneree
dry cleaner	**le pressing**	luh praysing
confectioner	**le confiseur**	luh koñfeesur
cheese shop	**la fromagerie**	lah fromajeree

❸ *tobacconist*

❻ *bookshop*

❾ *bank*

4 Useful phrases

Familiarize yourself with these phrases.

Where is the hairdresser?	**Où est le coiffeur?**	oo ay luh kwafur
Where do I pay?	**Je dois payer où?**	juh dwah payay oo
I'm just looking, thank you.	**Je regarde, merci.**	juh rugard, mairsee
Do you sell phonecards?	**Vous vendez des télécartes?**	voo vonday day telaykart
I'd like two of these.	**J'en veux deux.**	joñ vuh duh
Is there a department store in town?	**Il y a un grand magasin en ville?**	eelyah uñ groñ magazañ oñ veel
Can I place an order?	**Je peux passer une commande?**	juh puh passay oon komond

5 Say it

Where is the bank?

Do you sell cheese?

Where do I pay?

What is French for 40, 56, 77, 82, and 94? (pp.30–1)

Say "I'd like a big room". (pp.64–5)

Ask "Do you have a small car?" (pp.64–5)

Au marché
At the market

France uses the metric system of weights and measures. You need to ask for produce in kilogrammes or grammes. You may find that the older generation still use the term **une livre** (*a pound*) meaning half a kilo. Some larger items such as melons are sold individually **à la pièce**.

2 Match and repeat

Match the numbered items in this scene with the text in the panel.

1 **les courgettes** *(f)*
lay korjet

2 **la salade**
lah sah-lad

3 **les citrons** *(m)*
lay sitroñ

4 **les poireaux** *(m)*
lay pwaroe

5 **les tomates** *(f)*
lay toemat

6 **les champignons** *(m)*
lay shoñpeeyoñ

7 **les avocats** *(m)*
lay zavokah

8 **les pommes de terre** *(f)*
lay pom duh tair

1 *courgettes*

tomatoes **5**

mushrooms **6**

8 *potatoes*

7 *avocados*

3 In conversation

Je voudrais des tomates.
juh voodray day toemat

I'd like some tomatoes.

Des grosses ou des petites?
day gros oo day puhteet

The large ones or the small ones?

Deux kilos de grosse, s'il vous plaît.
duh keeloe duh gros, seel voo play

Two kilos of the large ones, please.

Cultural tip France now uses the common European currency, the euro. This is divided into 100 cents, which the French call "centimes" after the old divisions of the franc. You will usually hear the price given as: dix euros, vingt (€10.20), six euros, soixante-treize (€6.73), etc.

2 *lettuce*

3 *lemons*

4 *leeks*

4 Useful phrases

Learn these phrases. Then cover up the answers on the right. Read the English under the pictures and say the phrase in French as shown on the right.

The goat's cheese is too expensive.

Le fromage de chèvre est trop cher.
luh fromarj duh shevruh ay troe shair

How much is that cheese?

C'est combien ce fromage?
say koñbyañ suh fromarj

5 Say it

Three kilos of potatoes, please.

The mushrooms are too expensive.

How much is the lettuce?

That'll be all.

Ce sera tout.
suh surah too

Et avec ceci, madame.
ay avek susee, ma-dam

Anything else, madam.

Ce sera tout, merci. C'est combien?
suh surah too, mairsee. say koñbyañ

That'll be all, thank you. How much?

Trois euros, cinquante.
trwah zuroh, sankont

Three euros, fifty.

1 Warm up

What are these items you could buy in a supermarket (pp.24–5)?

la viande
le poisson
le fromage
le jus de fruits
le vin
l'eau

Au supermarché
At the supermarket

Prices in supermarkets are usually lower than in smaller shops. They offer all kinds of products, with the larger out-of-town **hypermarchés** (*hypermarkets*) extending to clothes, household goods, garden furniture, and DIY products. They may also stock regional products.

2 Match and repeat

Look at the numbered items and match them to the French words in the panel on the left.

1 **les produits d'entretien** *(m)*
lay prodwee doñtruh-tiañ

2 **les fruits** *(m)*
lay froo-wee

3 **les boissons** *(m)*
lay bwassoñ

4 **les plats préparés** *(m)*
lay plah prayparay

5 **les légumes** *(m)*
lay laygoom

6 **les produits surgelés** *(m)*
lay prodwee surjulay

7 **les produits laitiers** *(m)*
lay prodwee letyay

8 **les produits de beauté** *(m)*
lay prodwee duh boetay

household products ❶
fruit ❷
drinks ❸
ready meals ❹
vegetables ❺
frozen foods ❻

Cultural tip Fruit and vegetables sold by the kilo are usually weighed and priced at a separate counter. Alternatively, there may sometimes be a self-service weighing machine.

3 Useful phrases

Learn these phrases and then test yourself using the cover flap.

	May I have a bag, please?	**Je peux avoir un sac, s'il vous plaît?** juh puh avwar uñ sak, seel voo play
	Where is the drinks aisle?	**Où est le rayon des boissons?** oo ay luh rayonn day bwassoñ
	Where is the check-out, please?	**Où est la caisse, s'il vous plaît?** oo ay lah kes, seel voo play
	Please key in your pin.	**Tapez votre code, s'il vous plaît.** tapay votruh kod, seel voo play

4 Words to remember

Learn these words and then test yourself using the cover flap.

8 *beauty products*

7 *dairy products*

bread	**le pain** luh pañ
milk	**le lait** luh lay
butter	**le beurre** luh bur
ham	**le jambon** luh joñboñ
salt	**le sel** luh sel
pepper	**le poivre** luh pwavruh
washing powder	**la lessive** lah leseev
toilet paper	**le papier toilette** luh papyay twalet
nappies	**les couches** (f) lay koosh
washing-up liquid	**le liquide vaisselle** luh likeed vaysel

5 Say it

Where's the dairy products aisle?

May I have some ham, please?

Where are the frozen foods?

1 Warm up

Say "I'd like…".
(pp.22–3)

Ask "Do you have…?"
(pp.14–15)

Say "38", "42", and
"46". (pp.30–1)

Say "large", "small",
"bigger", and
"smaller". (pp.64–5)

Vêtements et chaussures
Clothes and shoes

Clothes and shoes are measured in
metric sizes. Even allowing for
conversion of sizes, French clothes
tend to be cut smaller than English
ones. Note that clothes size is **la taille**
but shoe size is **la pointure**.

2 Match and repeat

Match the numbered items of clothing to the French words in the
panel on the left. Use the cover flap to test yourself.

1 **la chemise**
   lah shumeez

2 **la cravate**
   lah kravat

3 **la veste**
   lah vest

4 **la poche**
   lah posh

5 **la manche**
   lah moñsh

6 **le pantalon**
   luh poñtaloñ

7 **la jupe**
   lah joop

8 **le collants** *(m)*
   luh kolloñ

9 **les chaussures** *(f)*
   lay shohsyur

shirt **1**

tie **2**

jacket **3**

pocket **4**

sleeve **5**

trousers **6**

🇫🇷 **Cultural tip** Like most of Europe,
France uses the continental system of sizes.
Dress sizes usually range from 36
(UK 8, US 6) through to 46 (UK
20, US 18) and shoe sizes from
37 (UK 4½, US 6) to 45 (UK 11, US
12). For men's shirts, a size
41 is a 16-inch collar, 43 is
a 17-inch collar, and 45
is an 18-inch collar.

3 Useful phrases

Learn these phrases and then test yourself using the cover flap.

Do you have a larger size?

Vous avez une taille plus grande?
voo zavay oon tie ploo groñd

It's not what I want.

Ce n'est pas ce que je veux.
suh nay pah sukuh juh vuh

I'll take the pink one.

Je prends la rose.
juh proñ lah roz

4 Words to remember

Colours are adjectives (pp.64–5) and often have a masculine, feminine, and plural form. The feminine is usually formed by adding an "e" and the plural by adding an "s".

red	**rouge/rouge**	rooj/rooj
white	**blanc/blanche**	bloñ/blonsh
blue	**bleu/bleue**	bluh/bluh
yellow	**jaune/jaune**	jon/jon
green	**vert/verte**	vair/vairt
black	**noir/noire**	nwar/nwar

❼ *skirt*

❽ *tights*

❾ *shoes*

5 Say it

I'll take the yellow one.

Do you have this jacket in black?

I'd like a 38.

Do you have a smaller size?

Réponses
Answers
Cover with flap

Révisez et répétez
Review and repeat

1 Market

1 **les tomates**
lay toemat

2 **les champignons**
lay shoñpeeyoñ

3 **les pommes de terre**
lay pom duh tair

4 **les courgettes**
lay korjet

5 **la salade**
lah sah-lad

6 **les avocats**
lay zavokah

1 Market

Name the numbered vegetables in French.

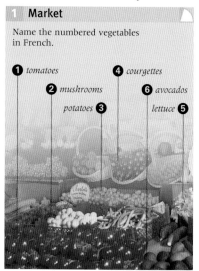

1 *tomatoes* 4 *courgettes*
2 *mushrooms* 6 *avocados*
potatoes 3 *lettuce* 5

2 Description

1 *These shoes are too expensive.*

2 *My room is very small.*

3 *I need a softer bed.*

2 Description

What do these sentences mean?

1 **Ces chaussures sont trop chères.**

2 **Ma chambre est très petite.**

3 **J'ai besoin d'un lit plus mou.**

3 Shops

1 **la boulangerie**
lah booloñjuree

2 **l'épicerie**
laypeesree

3 **la librairie**
lah leebrairee

4 **la poissonnerie**
lah pwasoñree

5 **la pâtisserie**
lah pateesree

6 **la boucherie**
lah boosheree

3 Shops

Name the numbered shops in French then check your answers.

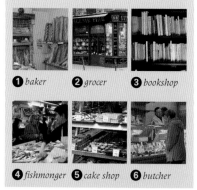

1 *baker* 2 *grocer* 3 *bookshop*

4 *fishmonger* 5 *cake shop* 6 *butcher*

4 Supermarket

What is the French for the numbered product categories?

❶ household products

❷ beauty products

❸ drinks

❹ dairy products

❺ frozen foods

4 Supermarket

1 **les produits d'entretien**
lay prodwee doñtruh-tiañ

2 **les produits de beauté**
lay prodwee duh boetay

3 **les boissons**
lay bwassoñ

4 **les produits laitiers**
lay prodwee letyay

5 **les produits surgelés**
lay prodwee surjulay

5 Museum

Follow this conversation replying in French following the English prompts.

Bonjour. Je peux vous aider?
1 *Three adults and two children.*

Ça fait soixante-dix euros.
2 *That's very expensive!*

Nous ne faisons pas de réductions pour les enfants.
3 *How much is a guide?*

Quinze euros.
4 *Five tickets and a guide, please.*

Quatre-vingt-cinq euros, s'il vous plaît.
5 *Here you are. Where are the toilets?*

Là-bas.
6 *Thank you very much.*

5 Museum

1 **Trois adultes et deux enfants.**
trwah zadoolt ay duh zoñfoñ

2 **C'est très cher!**
say tray shair

3 **C'est combien pour un guide?**
say koñbyañ poor uñ geed

4 **Cinq entrées et un guide, s'il vous plaît**
sank oñtray ay tuñ geed, seel voo play

5 **Voilà. Où sont les toilettes?**
vwalah. oo soñ lay twalet

6 **Merci beaucoup.**
mairsee bohkoo

1 Warm up

Ask "which platform?" (pp.38–9)

What is the French for the following family members: "sister", "brother", "mother", "father", "son", and "daughter"? (pp.10–11)

Occupations
Jobs

Some occupations have a different form when the person is female – for example, **infirmier** (*male nurse*) and **infirmière** (*female nurse*). Others such as **professeur** remain the same for men and women. When you say your occupation, you don't use **un/une** (*a*) as in **Je suis avocat** (*I'm a lawyer*).

2 Words to remember: jobs

Familiarize yourself with these occupations and test yourself using the flap. The feminine form is shown in parentheses.

médecin medsañ	*doctor*
dentiste doñteest	*dentist*
infirmier(ière) añfairmyay(yair)	*nurse*
professeur profesur	*teacher*
comptable koñtabluh	*accountant*
avocat(e) avokah(aht)	*lawyer*
designer deesienur	*designer*
consultant(e) koñsooltoñ(oñt)	*consultant*
secrétaire sekraytair	*secretary*
commerçant(e) komairsoñ(oñt)	*shopkeeper*
électricien(ne) aylektreesyañ(en)	*electrician*
plombier ploñbyay	*plumber*
cuisinier(ière) kweeseenyay(yair)	*cook/chef*
ingénieur añjaynyur	*engineer*
à mon compte ah moñ kont	*self-employed*

Je suis plombier.
juh swee ploñbyay
I'm a plumber.

Elle est professeur.
el ay profesur
She is a teacher.

3 Put into practice

Join in the conversation. Conceal the text on the right with the cover flap and complete the dialogue in French.

Quelle est votre profession?
kel ay votruh profesyoñ
What do you do?

Say: I am a consultant.

Je suis consultant.
juh swee koñsooltoñ

Vous travaillez pour quelle compagnie?
voo trav-eyeyay poor kel koñpanee
What company do you work for?

Say: I'm self-employed.

Je suis à mon compte.
juh swee ah moñ kont

Comme c'est intéressant!
kom say añtayraysoñ
How interesting!

Ask: What is your profession?

Et quelle est votre profession?
ay kel ay votruh profesyoñ

Je suis dentiste.
juh swee doñteest
I'm a dentist.

Say: My sister is a dentist too.

Ma sœur est dentiste aussi.
mah sur ay doñteest ohsee

4 Words to remember: workplace

Familiarize yourself with these words and test yourself.

Le siège social est à Lille.
luh syej sosyal ay tah leel
Head office is in Lille.

head office	**le siège social** luh syej sosyal
branch	**lah succursale** lah sookoorsal
department	**le département** luh daypartumoñ
reception	**la réception** lah resepsyoñ
manager	**le chef** luh shef
trainee	**le stagiaire** luh stajyair

Practise different ways of introducing yourself in different situations (pp.8–9). Mention your name, occupation, nationality, and any other information you'd like to volunteer.

Le bureau
The office

An office environment or business situation has its own vocabulary in any language, but there are many items for which the terminology is virtually universal. Be aware that French computer keyboards have a different layout to the standard English QWERTY convention.

Familiarize yourself with these words. Read them aloud several times and try to memorize them. Conceal the French with the cover flap and test yourself.

le moniteur luh moneetur	*monitor*
l'ordinateur *(m)* lordeenatur	*computer*
la souris lah sooree	*mouse*
l'email *(m)* leemail	*e-mail*
l'internet *(m)* lañtairnet	*internet*
le mot de passe luh moh duh pas	*password*
la messagerie téléphonique lah mesah-juree telayfoneek	*voicemail*
le fax luh fax	*fax machine*
le copieur luh kopee-ur	*photocopier*
l'agenda *(m)* lajeñdah	*diary*
la carte de visite lah kart duh veezeet	*business card*
la réunion lah rayoonyon	*meeting*
la conférence lah konfayroñs	*conference*
l'ordre du jour *(m)* lordruh doo joor	*agenda*

1 *lamp*

screen **4**

2 *stapler*

telephone **3**

pen **10**

notepad **11**

drawer **12**

3 Useful phrases

Learn these phrases and then test yourself using the cover flap.

	I need to make some photocopies.	**J'ai besoin de faire des photocopies.** jay buzwañ duh fair day fotokopee
	I'd like to arrange an appointment.	**Je voudrais prendre rendez-vous.** juh voodray proñdruh roñday-voo
	I want to send an e-mail.	**Je veux envoyer un email.** juh vuh oñvwayay uñ eemail

4 Match and repeat

Match the numbered items to the French words on the right.

5 *keyboard*

6 *laptop*

printer 9

7 *desk*

8 *clock*

13 *swivel chair*

1 **la lampe** lah lomp

2 **l'agrafeuse** *(f)* lagrafurz

3 **le téléphone** luh telayfon

4 **l'écran** *(m)* laykroñ

5 **le clavier** luh klaveeyay

6 **l'ordinateur portable** *(m)* lordeenatur portabluh

7 **le bureau** luh byuroh

8 **la pendule** lah poñdool

9 **l'imprimante** *(f)* lampreemont

10 **le stylo** luh steeloh

11 **le bloc-notes** luh blok-not

12 **le tiroir** luh teerwar

13 **la chaise tournante** lah shayz toornont

5 Say it

I'd like to arrange a conference.

I need to send a fax.

Do you have a laptop?

1 Warm up

Say "How interesting!" (p.78–9), "library" (pp.48–9), and "traffic lights". (pp.50–1)

Ask "What is your profession?" and answer "I'm an engineer". (pp.78–9)

Le monde académique
Academic world

In France **une licence** (*batchelor's degree*) generally takes three years, followed by **une maîtrise** (*master's degree*) and **un doctorat** (*PhD*). Paris has several universities, often referred to by Roman numerals, as in Paris V.

2 Useful phrases

Familiarize yourself with these phrases and then test yourself.

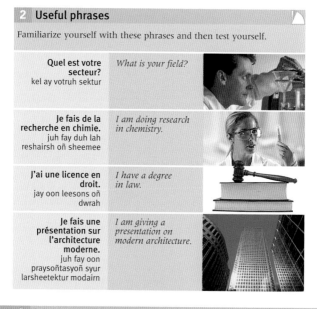

Quel est votre secteur? kel ay votruh sektur	*What is your field?*
Je fais de la recherche en chimie. juh fay duh lah reshairsh oñ sheemee	*I am doing research in chemistry.*
J'ai une licence en droit. jay oon leesons oñ dwrah	*I have a degree in law.*
Je fais une présentation sur l'architecture moderne. juh fay oon praysoñtasyoñ syur larsheetektur modairn	*I am giving a presentation on modern architecture.*

3 In conversation

Bonjour, je suis professeur Stein.
boñjoor, juh swee profesur stayeen

Hello, I'm Professor Stein.

De quelle université êtes-vous?
duh kel ooneevair-sitay et voo

What university are you from?

Je suis déléguée de l'université Paris II.
juh swee daylaygay duh looneevair-sitay paree duh

I'm the delegate from Paris II University.

4 Words to remember

Familiarize yourself with these words and then test yourself.

conference	**la conférence**	lah koñfayroñs
trade fair	**la foire-exposition**	lah fwar-ekspohseesyoñ
seminar	**le séminaire**	luh semeenair
lecture theatre	**l'amphithéâtre** (m)	loñfeetayatruh
conference room	**la salle de conférences**	lah sal duh koñfayroñs
exhibition	**l'exposition** (f)	lekspohzeesyoñ
library	**la bibliothèque**	lah biblee-yotek
university lecturer	**le maître de conférences**	luh metruh duh koñfayroñs
professor	**le professeur**	luh profesur
medicine	**la médecine**	lah medseen
science	**la science**	lah siyons
literature	**la littérature**	lah leetairatyur
engineering	**l'ingénierie** (f)	lahjayneeuree

Nous avons un stand à la foire-exposition.
noo zavon uñ stond ah lah fwar ekspohseesyoñ
We have a stand at the trade fair.

5 Say it

I'm doing research in medicine.

I have a degree in literature.

She's the professor.

Quel est votre secteur?
kel ay votruh sektur

What's your field?

Je fais de la recherche en ingénierie.
juh fay duh lah reshairsh oñ lahjayneeuree

I'm doing research in engineering.

Comme c'est intéressant.
kom say añtayraysoñ

How interesting.

Les affaires
In business

1 Warm up

Ask "Can I ...?"
(pp.34–5)

Say "I want to send an
e-mail". (pp.80–1)

Ask "Can you send an
e-mail?" (pp.80–1)

You will receive a more friendly
reception and make a good impression
if you make the effort to begin a
meeting with a short introduction in
French, even if your vocabulary is
limited. After that, all parties will
probably be happy to continue the
meeting in English.

2 Words to remember

Familiarize yourself with these words and
then test yourself by concealing the French
with the cover flap.

le client
luh kleeyoñ
client

le planning luh planning	*schedule*
la livraison lah leevraysoñ	*delivery*
le paiement luh paymoñ	*payment*
le budget luh bujay	*budget*
le prix luh pree	*price*
le document luh dokoomoñ	*document*
la facture lah faktyur	*invoice*
le devis luh duhvees	*estimate*
les bénéfices *(m)* lay baynayfees	*profits*
les ventes *(f)* lay vont	*sales*
les chiffres *(m)* lay sheefruh	*figures*

Cultural tip In general, commercial
dealings are formal, but a lunch with wine is
still part of doing business in France. As a
client, you can expect to be taken out to a
restaurant and as a supplier you should
consider entertaining your customers.

3 Useful phrases

Memorize these phrases. Note that when asking *what...?* you use
quel(s) with masculine words but **quelle(s)** with feminine words.

On signe le contrat?
oñ seenuh luh koñtrah
*Shall we sign the
contract?*

le cadre
luh kadruh
executive

le contrat
luh koñtrah
contract

*Please send me the
contract.*

**Envoyez-moi le
contrat s'il vous plaît.**
oñvwayay mwah luh
koñtrah, seel voo play

**Nous sommes
convenus d'un
planning?**
noo som koñvunoo
duñ planning

*Have we agreed a
schedule?*

**Quand pouvez-vous
faire la livraison?**
koñ poovay voo fair lah
leevraysoñ

*When can you make
the delivery?*

Quel est le budget?
kel ay luh bujay

What's the budget?

**Vous pouvez
m'envoyer la facture?**
voo poovay moñvwayay
lah faktyur

*Can you send me the
invoice?*

le rapport
luh rapor
report

4 Say it

Can you send me the estimate?

Have we agreed a price?

What are the profits?

Révisez et répétez
Review and repeat

1 At the office

1 l'agraffeuse
  lagrafurz

2 la lampe
  lah lomp

3 l'ordinateur
  portable
  lordeenatur
  portabluh

4 le stylo
  luh steeloh

5 le bureau
  luh byuroh

6 le bloc-notes
  luh blok-not

7 la pendule
  lah poñdool

1 At the office

Name these items.

- 2 *lamp*
- 3 *laptop*
- 4 *pen*
- 1 *stapler*
- 5 *desk*
- 6 *notepad*

2 Jobs

1 médecin
  medsañ

2 plombier
  ploñbyay

3 commerçant
  comairsoñ(oñt)

4 comptable
  koñtabluh

5 professeur
  profesur

6 avocat
  avokah(aht)

2 Jobs

What are these jobs in French?

1 *doctor*

2 *plumber*

3 *shopkeeper*

4 *accountant*

5 *teacher*

6 *lawyer*

clock **7**

3 Work

Answer these questions following the English prompts.

Vous travaillez pour quelle compagnie?
1 *Say "I work for myself".*

De quelle université êtes-vous?
2 *Say "I'm at the University of Bordeaux".*

Quel est votre secteur?
3 *Say "I'm doing medical research".*

Nous sommes convenus d'un planning?
4 *Say "Yes. Can you send me the budget?"*

3 Work

1 **Je suis à mon compte.**
juh swee zah moñ koñt

2 **Je suis de l'université de Bordeaux.**
juh swee duh looneevair-sitay duh bordoe

3 **Je fais de la recherche en médecine.**
juh fay duh lah reshairsh oñ medseen

4 **Oui. Vous pouvez m'envoyer le budget?**
voo poovay moñvwayay luh bujay

4 How much?

Answer the question with the amount shown in brackets.

1 **C'est combien le café?** (€2.50)

2 **C'est combien la chambre?** (€47)

3 **C'est combien pour un kilo de tomates?** (€3.25)

4 **C'est combien l'emplacement pour quatre jours?** (€50)

4 How much?

1 **C'est deux euros cinquante.**
say duh zuroh sankont

2 **C'est quarante-sept euros.**
say sankont-set uroh

3 **C'est trois euros vingt-cinq**
say twrah zuroh vañ-sank

4 **C'est cinquante euros.**
say sankont uroh

A la pharmacie
At the chemist

Say "I'm allergic to nuts". (pp.24–5)

Say the verb "avoir" (to have) in all its forms (je, tu, il/elle, vous, nous, ils/elles). (pp.14–15)

French pharmacists study for seven years before qualifying. They can give advice about minor health problems and are permitted to dispense a wide variety of medicines, even giving injections, if necessary. There is a duty pharmacist (**pharmacie de garde**) in most towns.

2 Match and repeat

Match the numbered items to the French words in the panel on the left and test yourself using the flap.

1 **le bandage**
luh boñdarj

2 **le sirop**
luh seeroe

3 **les gouttes** *(f)*
lay goot

4 **le pansement**
luh poñsumoñ

5 **la seringue**
lah surañg

6 **la crème**
lah krem

7 **le suppositoire**
luh soopozitwar

8 **le cachet**
luh kashay

bandage **1**   *syrup* **2**

drops **3**

plaster **4**   *syringe* **5**

3 In conversation

Bonjour madame, vous désirez?
boñjoor, mad-dam. voo dayzeeray

Hello madam. What would you like?

J'ai mal à l'estomac.
jay mal ah lestomah

I have a stomach ache.

Vous avez la diarrhée?
voo zavay lah dyaray

Do you have diarrhoea?

4 Words to remember

Familiarize yourself with these words and test yourself using the flap.

J'ai mal à la tête.
jay mal ah lah tet
I have a headache.

headache	**mal à la tête**	mal ah lah tet
stomach ache	**mal à l'estomac**	mal ah lestomah
diarrhoea	**la diarrhée**	lah dyaray
cold	**un rhume**	uñ room
cough	**une toux**	oon too
sunburn	**un coup de soleil**	uñ koo duh sol-lay
toothache	**mal aux dents**	mal oh doñ

6 Say it

I have a cold.

Do you have that as a cream?

Do you have a cough?

6 *cream*

7 *suppository*

8 *tablet*

5 Useful phrases

Familiarize yourself with these phrases and then test yourself using the cover flap.

I have sunburn.	**J'ai un coup de soleil.**	jay uñ koo duh sol-lay
Do you have that as tablets?	**Vous avez des cachets à la place?**	voo zavay day kashay ah lah plas
I'm allergic to penicillin.	**Je suis allergique à la pénicilline.**	juh swee zalurgeek ah lah peneesilin

Non, mais j'ai aussi mal à la tête.
noñ, may jay osee mal ah lah tet

No, but I also have a headache.

Prenez ça.
prunay sah

Take this.

Vous avez un sirop à la place?
voo zavay uh seeroe ah lah plas

Do you have that as a syrup?

1 Warm up

Say " I have a toothache" and "I have sunburn". (pp.88–9)

Say the French for "red", "green", "black", and "yellow". (pp.74–5)

Le corps
The body

The most common phrase for talking about aches and pains is **J'ai mal à…** Don't forget that when **à** is placed in front of **le** it becomes **au** and in front of **les** it becomes **aux** (the "x" is silent). For example, **J'ai mal au dos** (*I have a backache*) and **J'ai mal aux oreilles** (*I have earache*).

2 Match and repeat: body

Match the numbered parts of the body with the list on the left. Test yourself by using the cover flap.

1 **la main**
lah mañ

2 **la tête**
lah tet

3 **l'épaule** *(f)*
laypoll

4 **le coude**
luh kood

5 **les cheveux**
lay shuhvuh

6 **le bras**
luh brah

7 **le cou**
luh koo

8 **la poitrine**
lah pwatreen

9 **l'estomac** *(m)*
lestomah

10 **la jambe**
lah jomb

11 **le genou**
luh juhnoo

12 **le pied**
luh piyay

hand ❶
head ❷
shoulder ❸
❹ *elbow*
❺ *hair*
❻ *arm*
❼ *neck*
❽ *chest*
❾ *stomach*
❿ *leg*
⓫ *knee*
⓬ *foot*

3 Match and repeat: face

Match the numbered facial features with the list on the right.

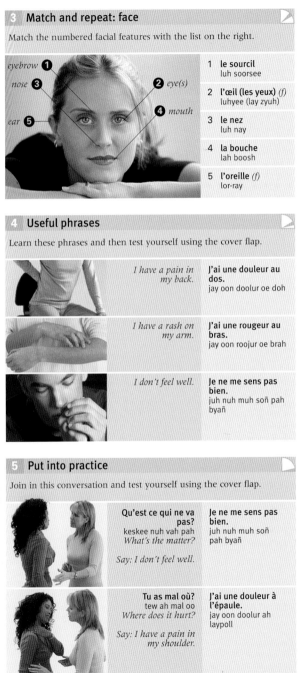

eyebrow **1**

nose **3**

2 eye(s)

4 mouth

ear **5**

1 **le sourcil**
luh soorsee

2 **l'œil (les yeux)** *(f)*
luhyee (lay zyuh)

3 **le nez**
luh nay

4 **la bouche**
lah boosh

5 **l'oreille** *(f)*
lor-ray

4 Useful phrases

Learn these phrases and then test yourself using the cover flap.

I have a pain in my back.

J'ai une douleur au dos.
jay oon doolur oe doh

I have a rash on my arm.

J'ai une rougeur au bras.
jay oon roojur oe brah

I don't feel well.

Je ne me sens pas bien.
juh nuh muh soñ pah byañ

5 Put into practice

Join in this conversation and test yourself using the cover flap.

Qu'est ce qui ne va pas?
keskee nuh vah pah
What's the matter?

Say: *I don't feel well.*

Je ne me sens pas bien.
juh nuh muh soñ pah byañ

Tu as mal où?
tew ah mal oo
Where does it hurt?

Say: *I have a pain in my shoulder.*

J'ai une douleur à l'épaule.
jay oon doolur ah laypoll

1 Warm up

Say "I need some tablets" and "He needs some cream". (pp.60–1 and pp.88–9)

What is the French for "I don't have a son"? (pp.10–15)

Chez le docteur
At the doctor

Unless it's an emergency, you have to book an appointment with the doctor and pay when you leave. You can usually reclaim the money if you have medical insurance. You can find the names and addresses of local doctors from the local town hall or **syndicat d'initiative** (*tourist office*).

2 Useful phrases you may hear

Familiarize yourself with these phrases and then test yourself using the cover flap to conceal the French on the left.

Ce n'est pas sérieux. suh nay pah seryuh	*It's not serious.*
Vous avez besoin de tests. voo zavay buzwañ duh test	*You need to have tests.*
Vous avez une infection aux reins. voo zavay oon añfeksyoñ oh rañ	*You have a kidney infection.*
Vous avez besoin d'aller à l'hôpital. voo zavay buzwañ dalay ah lopeetal	*You need to go to hospital.*

Vous prenez des médicaments? voo prunay day maydikamoñ
Are you taking any medications?

3 In conversation

Qu'est-ce qui ne va pas? keskee nuh vah pah

What's the matter?

J'ai une douleur à la poitrine. jay oon doolur ah lah pwatreen

I have a pain in my chest.

Laissez-moi vous examiner. lessay-mwah voo zekzaminay

Let me examine you.

Cultural tip If you are an EU national, you are entitled to free emergency medical treatment in France on production of a European Health Insurance Card or E111 form. For an ambulance call 15.

4 Useful phrases you may need to say

Practise these phrases and then test yourself using the cover flap.

I'm diabetic.	**Je suis diabétique.** juh swee diyabeteek
I'm epileptic.	**Je suis épileptique.** juh swee zepeelepteek
I'm asthmatic.	**Je suis asthmatique.** juh swee zasmateek
I have a heart condition.	**J'ai un problème au cœur.** jay uñ prob-lem oh kur
I feel faint.	**Je vais m'évanouir.** juh vay mayvanoower
I have a fever.	**J'ai de la fièvre.** jay duh lah fyevruh
It's urgent.	**C'est urgent.** say turjoñ

Je suis enceinte.
juh swee zoñsant
I'm pregnant.

5 Say it

Do I need tests?

My son needs to go to hospital.

It's not urgent.

C'est sérieux?
say seryuh

Is it serious?

Non, vous avez seulement une indigestion.
noñ, voo zavay surlmoñ oon añdeejestyoñ

No, you only have indigestion.

Quel soulagement!
kel soolarjemoñ

What a relief!

1 Warm up

Ask "How long is the journey?" (pp.42–3)

How do you ask "Do I need...?" (pp.92–3)

What is the French for "mouth" and "head"? (pp.90–1)

A l'hôpital
At the hospital

The main hospitals in France are attached to universities and are known as **Centres Hospitaliers Universitaires** (CHU). It is useful to know a few basic phrases relating to hospitals for use in an emergency or in case you need to visit a friend or colleague in hospital.

2 Useful phrases

Familiarize yourself with these phrases. Conceal the French with the cover flap and test yourself.

Quelles sont les heures de visite? kel soñ lay zur duh vizeet	*What are the visiting hours?*
Ça va prendre combien de temps? sah vah prondruh koñbyañ duh toñ	*How long will it take?*
Ça va faire mal? sah vah fair mal	*Will it hurt?*
Allongez-vous ici, s'il vous plaît. aloñjay voo zeesee, seel voo play	*Please lie down here.*
Vous ne devez pas manger. voo nuh duvay pah moñjay	*You must not eat.*
Ne bougez pas la tête. nuh boojay pah lah tet	*Don't move your head.*
Ouvrez la bouche, s'il vous plaît. oovray lah boosh, seel voo play	*Please open your mouth.*
Vous avez besoin d'une prise de sang. voo zavay buzwañ doon preez duh soñ	*You need a blood test.*

l'intraveineuse *(f)* lañtravaynurz *intravenous drip*

Ça va mieux? sah vah meeyuh *Are you feeling better?*

Où est la salle d'attente? oo ay lah sal datont *Where is the waiting room?*

3 Words to remember

Memorize these words and test yourself using the cover flap.

Votre radio est normale.
votruh radyoh ay normal
Your x-ray is normal.

emergency department	**la salle des urgences** lah sal day zurjoñs
children's ward	**le service de pédiatrie** luh survees duh paydyah-tree
operating theatre	**la salle d'opération** lah sal dopairasyoñ
x-ray department	**la salle de radiologie** lah sal duh radyo-lojee
waiting room	**la salle d'attente** lah sal datont
lift	**l'ascenseur** lasoñsur
stairs	**les escaliers** lay zeskalyay

4 Put into practice

Join in this conversation. Read the French on the left and follow the instructions to make your reply. Then test yourself by concealing the answers with the cover flap.

Vous avez une infection.
voo zavay oon añfeksyoñ
You have an infection.

Ask: Do I need tests?

J'ai besoin de tests?
jay buzwañ duh test

Tout d'abord, vous avez besoin d'une prise de sang.
too dabor, voo zavay buzwañ doon preez duh soñ
First you will need a blood test.

Ask: Will it hurt?

Ça va faire mal?
sah vah fair mal

5 Say it

Does he need a blood test?

Where is the children's ward?

Do I need an x-ray?

Non, ne vous inquiétez pas.
noñ, nuh voo zañkyatay pah
No. Don't worry.

Ask: How long will it take?

Ça va prendre combien de temps?
sah vah proñdruh koñbyañ duh toñ

Révisez et répétez
Review and repeat

Réponses
Answers
Cover with flap

1 The body

1 **la tête**
lah tet

2 **le bras**
luh brah

3 **la poitrine**
lah pwatreen

4 **l'estomac**
lestomah

5 **la jambe**
lah jomb

6 **le genou**
luh juhnoo

7 **le pied**
luh piyay

1 The body

Name the numbered body parts in French.

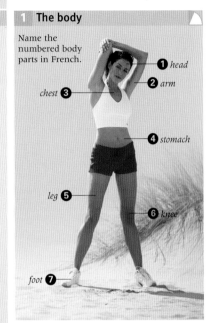

1 head
2 arm
chest 3
4 stomach
leg 5
6 knee
foot 7

2 On the phone

1 **Je voudrais parler à Caroline Martin.**
juh voodray parlay ah karoleen martañ

2 **[your name] de l'imprimerie Laporte.**
[your name] duh lahpreemuree laport

3 **Je peux laisser un message?**
juh puh laysay uñ mesarj

4 **C'est bon pour le rendez-vous lundi à onze heures.**
say boñ poor luh roñday-voo lañdee ah onz ur

5 **Merci, au revoir.**
mairsee, ovwar

2 On the phone

You are arranging an appointment. Follow the conversation, replying in French following the English prompts.

Allô, société Apex.
1 *I'd like to speak to Caroline Martin.*

Oui, c'est de la part de qui?
2 *[your name] of Laporte printers.*

Je suis désolé, la ligne est occupée.
3 *Can I leave a message?*

Oui, bien sûr.
4 *It's fine for the appointment on Monday at 11am.*

Très bien, au revoir.
5 *Thank you, goodbye.*

3 Clothing

Say the French words for the numbered items of clothing.

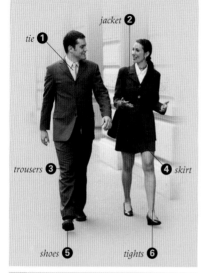

tie **1**

jacket **2**

trousers **3**

4 skirt

shoes **5**

tights **6**

3 Clothing

1 **la cravate**
lah kravat

2 **la veste**
lah vest

3 **le pantalon**
luh poñtaloñ

4 **la jupe**
lah joop

5 **les chaussures**
lay shohsyur

6 **les collants**
lay kolloñ

4 At the doctor's

Say these phrases in French.

1 *I don't feel well.*

2 *Do I need tests?*

3 *I have a heart condition.*

4 *Do I need to go to hospital?*

5 *I am pregnant.*

4 At the doctor's

1 **Je ne me sens pas bien.**
juh nuh muh soñ pah byañ

2 **J'ai besoin de tests.**
jay buzwañ duh test

3 **J'ai un problème au cœur.**
jay uñ prob-lem oh kur

4 **J'ai besoin d'aller à l'hôpital.**
jay buzwañ dallay ah lopeetal

5 **Je suis enceinte.**
juh swee zoñsant

Chez nous
At home

Many city-dwellers live in an apartment block (**l'immeuble**), but in rural areas the houses tend to be detached (**individuelle**). If you want to know the total number of rooms you will need to ask **"Combien de pièces?"**. If you want to know how many bedrooms, ask **"Combien de chambres?"**

1 Warm up

Say the months of the year in French. (pp.28–9)

Ask "Is there an art gallery?" (pp.48–9) and "How many brothers do you have?" (pp.14–15)

2 Match and repeat

Match the numbered items to the list and test yourself using the flap.

1 **la fenêtre**
lah fenaytruh

2 **la cheminée**
lah shemnay

3 **le toit**
lah twut

4 **la gouttière**
lah gootyair

5 **le mur**
luh myur

6 **le volet**
luh volay

7 **la porte**
lah port

8 **le passage**
luh passarj

window ❶   *chimney* ❷

❺ *wall*   ❻ *shutter*   *door* ❼

Cultural tip Most French houses have shutters ("volets") at each window. These are closed at night and in the heat of the day. Curtains, where they are present, tend to be more for decoration. A single-storey bungalow is known as "un pavillon" and these are popular among the French as holiday homes in tourist resorts.

3 Words to remember

Familiarize yourself with these words and test yourself using the flap.

Quel est le loyer par mois?
kel ay luh lwayay par mwah?
What is the rent per month?

room	**la pièce** lah pyes
floor	**le sol** luh sol
ceiling	**le plafond** luh plafoñ
bedroom	**la chambre** lah shombruh
bathroom	**la salle de bains** lah sal duh bañ
kitchen	**la cuisine** lah kwiseen
dining room	**la salle à manger** lah sal ah moñjay
living room	**le salon** luh saloñ
cellar	**la cave** lah kav
attic	**le grenier** luh grunyay

3 roof

4 gutter

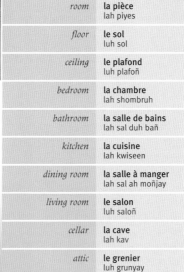

8 driveway

4 Useful phrases

Learn these phrases and test yourself.

Is there a garage?

Il y a un garage?
eelyah uh gararj

When is it available?

C'est disponible quand?
say deesponeebluh koñ

5 Say it

Is there a dining room?

Is it large?

Is it available in July?

Is it furnished?

C'est meublé?
say murblay

Dans la maison
In the house

What is the French for "room" (pp.58–9), "desk" (pp.80–1), "bed" (pp.60–1), and "toilet(s)"? (pp.52–3)

How do you say "soft", "beautiful", and "big"? (pp.64–5)

When you rent a house or villa in France, it is usual to be asked to pay for services such as electricity and gas in addition to the basic weekly or monthly rent. Additional charges might also extend to wood or other fuel for an open fire, which is usually charged by the cubic metre.

2 Match and repeat

Match the numbered items to the list in the panel on the left. Then test yourself by concealing the French with the cover flap.

❶ *worktop*

1 **le plan de travail**
luh plañ duh traveye

2 **l'évier** *(m)*
levyay

3 **le micro-ondes**
luh meekro-ond

4 **la cuisinière**
lah kwiseenyair

5 **le four**
luh foor

6 **le frigo**
luh freegoh

7 **la table**
lah tabluh

8 **la chaise**
lah shez

❺ *oven*

❻ *fridge*

❹ *cooker*

table ❼

3 In conversation

C'est le four.
say luh foor

This is the oven.

Il y a un lave-vaisselle aussi?
eelyah uñ lav-vaysel osee

Is there a dishwasher as well?

Oui, et il y a un grand congélateur.
wee, ay eelyah uñ groñ koñjelatur

Yes, and there's a big freezer.

4 Words to remember

Familiarize yourself with these words and test yourself using the flap.

wardrobe	**l'armoire** *(f)* larmwar
armchair	**le fauteuil** luh fohtuhee
chest of drawers	**la commode** lah komohd
fireplace	**la cheminée** lah shemnay
carpet	**le tapis** luh tapee
bathtub	**la baignoire** lah bainwar
wash basin	**le lavabo** luh lavabo
curtains	**les rideaux** *(m)* lay ridoe

Le canapé est neuf.
luh kanapay ay nurf
The sofa is new.

microwave ❸

❷ *sink*

❽ *chair*

5 Useful phrases

Practise these phrases and then test yourself using the cover flap to conceal the French.

Is electricity included?	**L'électricité est inclue?** laylektreesitay et añkloo
I don't like the curtains.	**Je n'aime pas les rideaux.** juh nem pah lay ridoe
The carpet is old.	**Le tapis est vieux.** luh tapee ay vyuh

6 Say it

Is there a microwave?

I like the fireplace.

What a soft sofa!

L'évier est neuf?
levyay ay nurf

Is the sink new?

Bien sûr. Et voilà la machine à laver.
byañ syur. ay vwalah lah masheen ah lavay

Of course. And here's the washing machine.

Quel beau carrelage!
kel boe karlarj

What beautiful tiles!

Say "I need", "you need", "he needs". (pp.64–5, pp.92–4)

What is the French for "day", "week", and "month"? (pp.28–9)

Say the days of the week. (pp.28–9)

Le jardin
The garden

The garden of a house or villa may be communal, or at least partly shared. Check with the estate agent. In general, French gardens are well-kept and reasonably formal. The natural, "wild" look is not very popular and hedges are usually carefully trimmed and lawns are regularly mown.

2 Words to remember

Familiarize yourself with these words and test yourself using the flap.

la tondeuse à gazon lah toñdurz ah gazoñ	*lawn mower*
la fourche lah foorsh	*fork*
la bêche lah besh	*spade*
le râteau luh ratoe	*rake*
la jardinerie lah jardañree	*garden centre*

❷ *tree*

❸ *soil*

terrace ❶

flowers ❼   *weeds* ❽   ❾ *path*

3 Useful phrases

Familarize yourself with these phrases and then test yourself.

	The gardener comes once a week.	**Le jardinier vient une fois par semaine.** luh jardañyay vyañ oon fwah par suhmayn
	Can you mow the lawn?	**Vous pouvez tondre la pelouse?** voo poovay toñdruh lah pelooz
	Is the garden private?	**Le jardin est privé?** luh jardañ ay preevay
	The garden needs watering.	**Le jardin a besoin d'eau.** luh jardañ ah buzwañ doe

4 Match and repeat

Match the numbered items to the words in the panel on the right.

4 *lawn* **5** *hedge* **6** *plants*

flowerbed **10**

1	**la terrasse** lah terass
2	**l'arbre** *(m)* larbruh
3	**la terre** lah tair
4	**la pelouse** lah pelooz
5	**la haie** lah ay
6	**les plantes** *(f)* lay ploñt
7	**les fleurs** *(f)* lay flur
8	**les mauvaises herbes** *(f)* lay movay zurb
9	**l'allée** *(f)* lallay
10	**le parterre de fleurs** luh partair duh flur

5 Say it

The lawn needs watering.

Are there any trees?

The gardener comes on Fridays.

Say "My name's John".
(pp.8–9)

How do you say "don't
worry"? (pp.94–5)

What's "your" in
French? (pp.12–13)

Les animaux
Pets

"Pet passports" are now available to
enable holiday-makers and
commuters to take their pets with
them to France and avoid quarantine
on return to the United Kingdom.
Consult your vet for details of how to
obtain the necessary vaccinations and
paperwork.

2   Match and repeat

Match the numbered animals to the French words
in the panel on the left. Then test yourself using
the cover flap.

1	**le chat** luh shah
2	**le lapin** luh lapañ
3	**l'oiseau** *(m)* lwazoe
4	**le poisson** luh pwassoñ
5	**le chien** luh shiañ
6	**le hamster** luh amstair

bird ❸
❷ *rabbit*
❶ *cat*
fish ❹
dog ❺
❻ *hamster*

3   Useful phrases

Familiarize yourself with these phrases and then
test yourself using the cover flap.

Ce chien est gentil? suh shiañ ay joñtee	*Is this dog friendly?*
Je peux amener mon chien? juh puh amunay moñ shiañ	*Can I bring my dog?*
J'ai peur des chats. jay pur day shah	*I'm frightened of cats.*
Mon chien ne mord pas. moñ shiañ nuh mor pah	*My dog doesn't bite.*

**Ce chat est plein
de puces.**
suh shah ay plañ
duh pous
This cat is full of fleas.

██ **Cultural tip** Many dogs in France are guard dogs and you may encounter them tethered or roaming free. Approach farms and rural houses with care, and keep away from the dog's territory. Look out for warning notices such as "Attention au chien" (Beware of the dog).

ATTENTION AU CHIEN

4 Words to remember

Memorize these words and test yourself using the cover flap.

vet	**le vétérinaire**	luh vetairinair
vaccination	**la vaccination**	lah vaksinasyoñ
pet passport	**le passeport d'animaux**	luh passpor danimoe
basket	**le panier**	luh panyay
cage	**la cage**	lah karj
bowl	**la gamelle**	lah gamel
collar	**le collier**	luh kolyay
lead	**la laisse**	lah less
fleas	**les puces** *(f)*	lay pous

Mon chien est malade.
moñ shiañ ay malahd
My dog is not well.

5 Put into practice

Join in this conversation. Read the French on the left and follow the instructions to make your reply. Then test yourself by concealing the answers with the cover flap.

C'est votre chien?
say votruh shiañ
Is this your dog?

Say: Yes, he's called Sandy.

Oui, il s'appelle Sandy.
wee, eel sapell Sandy

J'ai peur des chiens.
jay pur day shiañ
I'm frightened of dogs.

Say: Don't worry. He's friendly.

Ne vous inquiétez pas. Il est gentil.
nuh voo zañkyatay pah. eel ay joñtee

Révisez et répétez
Review and repeat

1 Colours

1 noir
nwar

2 blanche
blonsh

3 rouge
rooj

4 verte
vairt

5 jaunes
jon

1 Colours

Complete the sentences with the French for the colour in brackets. Be careful to choose the correct masculine or feminine form.

1 **Vous avez cette veste en _____ ?** *(black)*

2 **Je prends la jupe _____ .** *(white)*

3 **Vous avez cette robe en _____ ?** *(red)*

4 **Non mais j'ai une _____ .** *(green)*

5 **Vous avez des chaussettes _____ ?** *(yellow)*

2 Kitchen

1 la cuisinière
lah kwiseenyair

2 le frigo
luh freegoh

3 l'évier
levyay

4 le micro-ondes
luh meekro-ond

5 le four
luh foor

6 la chaise
lah shez

7 la table
lah tabluh

2 Kitchen

Say the French words for the numbered items.

❶ *cooker*

fridge ❷

oven ❺   *chair* ❻

3 House

You are visiting a house in France. Join in the conversation, replying in French following the English prompts.

Voilà le salon.
1 *What a lovely fireplace!*

Oui, et il y a aussi une grande cuisine.
2 *How many bedrooms?*

Il y a trois chambres.
3 *Do you have a garage?*

Non, mais il y a un grand jardin.
4 *When is it available?*

Juillet.
5 *What is the rent a month?*

3 House

1 **Quelle belle cheminée!**
kel bel shemnay

2 **Combien de chambres?**
koñbyañ duh shombruh

3 **Vous avez un garage?**
voo zavay uñ gararj

4 **C'est disponible quand?**
say deesponeebluh koñ

5 **Quel est le loyer par mois?**
kel ay luh lwayay par mwah

4 At home

Say the French for the following items:

1 *washing machine*
2 *sofa*
3 *attic*
4 *dining room*
5 *tree*
6 *garden*

microwave 4
3 sink
table 7

4 At home

1 **la machine à laver**
lah masheen ah lavay

2 **le canapé**
luh kanapay

3 **le grenier**
luh grunyay

4 **la salle à manger**
lah sal ah moñjay

5 **l'arbre**
larbruh

6 **le jardin**
luh jardañ

Ask "How do I get to the bank?" and "How do I get to the post office?" (pp.68–9)

What's the French for "passport"? (pp.54–5)

Ask "What time?" (pp.30–1)

La poste et la banque
Post and bank

The post office also serves as a bank. You do not need to queue at the cashier, as there are normally cashpoints available outside the building. Stamps are also available from **le tabac** (*bar/tobacconists*).

2 Words to remember: post

Familiarize yourself with these words and test yourself using the cover flap to conceal the French on the left.

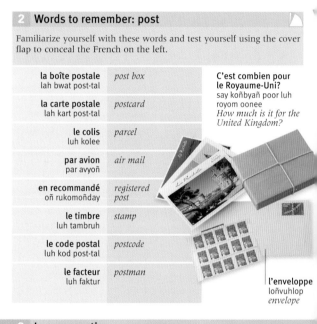

la boîte postale lah bwat post-tal	*post box*
la carte postale lah kart post-tal	*postcard*
le colis luh kolee	*parcel*
par avion par avyoñ	*air mail*
en recommandé oñ rukomoñday	*registered post*
le timbre luh tambruh	*stamp*
le code postal luh kod post-tal	*postcode*
le facteur luh faktur	*postman*

C'est combien pour le Royaume-Uni?
say koñbyañ poor luh royom oonee
How much is it for the United Kingdom?

l'enveloppe
loñvuhlop
envelope

3 In conversation

Je voudrais retirer de l'argent.
juh voodray ruteeray duh larjoñ

I'd like to withdraw some money.

Vous avez une identification?
voo zavay oon eedoñtee-fikasyoñ

Do you have any identification?

Oui, voilà mon passeport.
wee, vwalah moñ passpor

Yes, here's my passport.

4 Words to remember: bank

Familiarize yourself with these words and test yourself using the cover flap to conceal the French on the right.

la carte bancaire
lah kart boñkair
bank card

Comment je peux payer?
komon juh puh payay
How can I pay?

PIN	**le code**	luh kod
bank	**la banque**	lah boñk
cashier	**le guichet**	luh geeshay
notes	**les billets**	lay beeyay
ATM/cashpoint	**le distributeur automatique**	luh distreebootur otomateek
travellers' cheques	**les chèques de voyage**	lay shek duh vwoyarj

5 Useful phrases

Learn these phrases and then test yourself using the cover flap.

6 Say it

I'd like a stamp for the United Kingdom.

I'd like to change some travellers' cheques.

Do I need my passport?

I'd like to change some money.	**Je voudrais changer de l'argent.** juh voodray shoñjay duh larjoñ
What is the exchange rate?	**Quel est le taux de change?** kel ay luh toe duh shoñj
I'd like to withdraw some money.	**Je voudrais retirer de l'argent.** juh voodray ruteeray duh larjoñ

Composez votre code s'il vous plaît.
komposay votruh kod seel voo play

Please key in your PIN.

J'ai besoin de signer aussi?
jay buzwañ duh seenyay ohsee

Do I need to sign as well?

Non, ce n'est pas nécessaire.
noñ, suh nay pah nesesair

No, that's not necessary.

What's the French for "doesn't work"? (pp.60–1)

Say "today" and "tomorrow". (pp.28–9)

Les services
Services

You can combine the French words on these pages with the vocabulary you learned in week 10 to help you explain basic problems and cope with arranging most repairs. When organizing building work or a repair, it's a good idea to agree the price and method of payment in advance.

2 Words to remember

Familiarize yourself with these words and test yourself using the flap.

le plombier luh ploñbyay	*plumber*
l'électricien *(m)* laylektreesyañ	*electrician*
le garagiste luh gararjeest	*mechanic*
le constructeur luh koñstruktur	*builder*
la femme de ménage lah fam duh maynarj	*cleaner*
le décorateur luh daykoratur	*decorator*
le charpentier luh sharpañtyay	*carpenter*
le maçon luh massoñ	*bricklayer*

la manivelle
lah maneevel
wrench

Je n'ai pas besoin d'un garagiste.
juh nay pah buzwañ duñ gararjeest
I don't need a mechanic.

3 In conversation

La machine à laver est en panne.
lah masheen ah lavay ay toñ pan

The washing machine has broken down.

Oui, le tuyeau est cassé.
wee luh tweeyoh ay kassay

Yes, the hose is broken.

Vous pouvez la réparer?
voo poovay lah rayparay

Can you repair it?

4 Useful phrases

Learn these phrases and then test yourself using the cover flap.

Please clean the bathroom.	**Nettoyez la salle de bain, s'il vous plait.** netwuhyay lah sal duh bañ seel voo play
Can you repair the boiler?	**Vous pouvez réparer la chaudière?** voo poovay rayparay lah shodyair
Do you know a good electrician?	**Vous connaissez un bon électricien?** voo konessay uñ boñ aylektreesyañ

Je peux faire réparer ça où?
juh puh fair rayparay sah oo
Where can I get this repaired?

5 Put into practice

Practise these phrases. Cover up the text on the right and complete the dialogue in French. Check your answers and repeat if necessary.

Votre clôture est cassée.
votruh klotoor ay kassay
Your fence is broken.

Ask: Do you know a good builder?

Vous connaissez un bon constructeur?
voo konessay uh boñ koñstruktur

Oui, il y en a un dans le village.
wee, eelyonah uñ doñ luh villarj
Yes, there is one in the village.

Ask: Do you have his phone number?

Vous avez son numéro de téléphone?
voo zavay soñ noomairoe duh telayfon

Non, vous avez besoin d'un nouveau.
noñ. voo zavay buzwañ duñ noovoh

No, you need a new one.

Vous pouvez faire ça aujourd'hui?
voo poovay fair sah ohjoordwee

Can you do it today?

Non, je reviens demain.
non, juh ruvyañ dumañ

No. I'll come back tomorrow.

1 Warm up

Say the days of the week in French. (pp.28–9)

How do you say "cleaner"? (pp.110–11)

Say "It's 9.30", "10.45", and "12.00". (pp.10–11, pp.30–1)

Venir
To come

The verb **venir** (*to come*) is another important verb. Other useful verbs are made up of **venir** with a prefix, such **revenir** (*to come back*) and **devenir** (*to become*). These can be formed in the same way as **venir** (below). Remember that **je viens** can mean either *I come* or *I am coming*.

2 Venir: to come

Say the different forms of **venir** (*to come*) aloud. Use the cover flap to test yourself and, when you are confident, practise the sample sentences below.

je viens juh vyañ	*I come*
tu viens tew vyañ	*you come (informal singular)*
il/elle vient eel/el vyañ	*he/she comes*
nous venons noo vunoñ	*we come*
vous venez voo vunay	*you come (formal singular or plural)*
ils/elles viennent eel/el vyen	*they come*
Je viens de New York. juh vyañ duh noo york	*I come from New York.*
Nous venons tous les mardis. noo vunoñ too lay mardee	*We come every Tuesday.*
Ils viennent par le train. eel vyen par luh trañ	*They come by train.*

Il vient de Chine.
eel vyañ duh sheen
He comes from China.

🇫🇷 **Conversational tip** You can use the phrase "je viens de..." (literally "I come from...") to talk about something you have just done or have recently completed. For example "je viens de faire les courses" (I have just done the shopping) or "je viens d'envoyer un email" (I have just sent an e-mail). To say "just" in the sense of "only", as in "I eat just a sandwich for lunch", the French use "seulement": "je mange seulement un sandwich pour déjeuner".

3 Useful phrases

Learn these phrases and then test yourself using the cover flap.

When can I come?	**Je peux venir quand?** juh puh vuneer koñ
Where does she come from?	**Elle vient d'où?** el vyañ doo
The cleaner comes every Monday.	**La femme de ménage vient tous les lundis.** lah fam duh maynarj vyañ too lay luñdee
Come with me. (informal/formal)	**Viens avec moi./ Venez avec moi.** vyañ avek mwah/ vunay avek mwah

Je viens de me réveiller.
juh vyañ duh
muh rayvay-yay
I have just woken up.

4 Put into practice

Join in this conversation. Read the French on the left and follow the instructions to make your reply. Then test yourself by concealing the answers with the cover flap.

Bonjour, salon de coiffure Christine.
boñjoor, saloñ duh kwafur Christine
Hello, this is Christine's hair salon.

Say: I'd like an appointment.

Je voudrais un rendez-vous.
juh voodray uñ roñday-voo

Vous voulez venir quand?
voo voolay vuneer koñ
When do you want to come?

Say: Can I come today?

Je peux venir aujourd'hui?
juh puh vuneer oh-joordwee

Oui bien sûr, à quelle heure?
wee byañ syur, ah kel ur
Yes of course, what time?

Say: At 10.30.

A dix heures et demie.
ah deez ur ay dumee

1 Warm up

What's the French for "big/tall" and "small/short"? (pp.64–5)

Say "The room is big" and "The bed is small". (pp.64–5)

La police et le crime
Police and crime

While in France, if you are the victim of a crime, you report it to the police. In an emergency reach them by dialing 17. You may have to explain your problem in French, at least initially, so some basic vocabulary is useful. In the event of a burglary, the police will usually come to the house.

2 Words to remember: crime

Familiarize yourself with these words.

le cambriolage luh kañbryolarj	*burglary*
le rapport de police luh rapor duh polees	*police report*
le voleur luh volur	*thief*
la police lah polees	*police*
la déposition lah daypoziyoñ	*statement*
le témoin luh taymwañ	*witness*
l'avocat(e) lavokah(aht)	*lawyer*

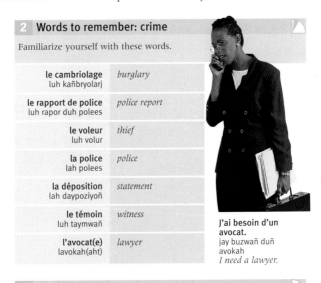

J'ai besoin d'un avocat.
jay buzwañ duñ avokah
I need a lawyer.

3 Useful phrases

Memorize these phrases and then test yourself using the cover flap.

J'ai été cambriolé(e). jay aytay kañbryolay	*I've been burgled.*
Qu'est-ce qui a été volé? keskee ah aytay volay	*What was stolen?*
Vous avez vu qui a fait ça? voo zavay voo kee ah fay sah	*Did you see who did it?*
Ça s'est passé quand? sah say passay koñ	*When did it happen?*

l'appareil-photo
lapareye foto
— *camera*

le porte-monnaie
luh port mohnay
purse

4 Words to remember: appearance

Learn these words. Remember some adjectives have a feminine form.

Il est chauve avec une barbe.
eel ay shohv avek oon barb
He is bald and has a beard.

Il a les cheveux noirs et courts.
eel ah lay shuvuh nwar ay kor
He has short, black hair.

man	**l'homme** *(m)*	lom
woman	**la femme**	lah fam
tall	**grand/grande**	groñ/groñd
short	**petit/petite**	puhtee/puhteet
young	**jeune**	juhn
old	**vieux/vieille**	vyuh/vyay
fat	**gros/grosse**	groe/gros
thin	**maigre**	maygruh
long/short hair	**les cheveux longs/ courts** *(m)*	lay shuvuh loñ/kor
spectacles	**les lunettes** *(f)*	lay loonet
beard	**la barbe**	lah barb

🇫🇷 Cultural tip In France there is a difference between "la gendarmerie" and "la police". La gendarmerie operates in smaller towns and la police in major cities. Their appearance and uniform are similar and officers from both forces carry guns.

5 Put into practice

Practise these phrases. Then cover up the text on the right and follow the instructions to make your reply in French.

Il ressemblait à quoi?
eel ruzoñblay ah kwah
What did he look like?

Say: *Short and fat.*

Petit et gros.
puhtee ay groe

Et les cheveux?
ay lay shuvuh
And the hair?

Say: *Long with a beard.*

Longs avec une barbe.
loñ avek oon barb

Révisez et répétez
Review and repeat

1 To come

1 **viens**
vyañ

2 **vient**
vyañ

3 **venons**
vunoñ

4 **venez**
vunay

5 **viennent**
vyen

1 To come

Put the correct form of **venir** (*to come*) into the gaps.

1 Je _____ à quatre heures.

2 Le jardinier _____ une fois par semaine.

3 Nous _____ pour déjeuner mardi.

4 Vous _____ avec nous?

5 Mes parents _____ par le train.

2 Bank and post

1 **les billets**
lay biyay

2 **les timbres**
lay tambruh

3 **la carte bancaire**
lah kart boñkair

4 **les cartes postales**
lay kart post-tal

5 **le colis**
luh kolee

2 Bank and post

Say the French words for the following numbered items:

❶ *notes*

❷ *stamps*

❸ *bank card*

❹ *postcards*

parcel ❺

3 Appearance

What do these descriptions mean?

1 C'est un homme grand et maigre.

2 Elle a les cheveux courts et des lunettes.

3 Je suis petite et j'ai les cheveux longs.

4 Elle est vieille et grosse.

5 Il a les yeux bleus et une barbe.

3 Appearance

1 *He's a tall thin man.*

2 *She has short hair and glasses.*

3 *I'm short and I have long hair.*

4 *She is old and fat.*

5 *He has blue eyes and a beard.*

4 The pharmacy

You are asking a pharmacist for advice. Join in the conversation, replying in French following the English prompts.

Bonjour. Je peux vous aider?
1 *I have a cough.*

Et vous avez aussi un rhume?
2 *No, but I have a headache.*

Prenez ces cachets.
3 *Do you have that as a syrup?*

Bien sûr. Voilà.
4 *Thank you. How much is that?*

Six euros.
5 *Here you are. Goodbye.*

4 The pharmacy

1 **J'ai une toux.**
jay oon too

2 **Non, mai j'ai mal à la tête.**
noñ. may jay mal ah lah tet

3 **Vous avez un sirop à la place?**
voo zavay uñ seeroe ah lah plas

4 **Merci. C'est combien?**
mairsee. say koñbyañ

5 **Voilà. Au revoir.**
vwalah. ovwar

1 Warm up

What is the French for "museum" and "art gallery"? (pp.48–9)

Say "I don't like the curtains". (pp.100–1)

Ask "Do you want…?" informally (pp.22–3)

Les loisirs
Leisure time

The French pride themselves on their support for the arts, including opera and film. It would not be unusual to number politics or philosophy among your interests. Phrasebooks aimed at French speakers often have a section on useful conversational openers for these topics.

2 Words to remember

Familiarize yourself with these words and test yourself using the cover flap to conceal the French on the left.

le théâtre luh tay-atruh	*theatre*
le cinéma luh sinaymah	*cinema*
la discothèque lah diskotek	*disco*
la musique lah moozeek	*music*
l'art (m) lar	*art*
le sport luh spor	*sport*
le tourisme luh torizmuh	*sightseeing*
les jeux vidéos lay juh viday-oh	*computer games*

J'adore l'opéra.
jador lopayra
I love opera.

les spectateurs (m)
lay spektahtur
audience

3 In conversation

Salut, tu veux jouer au tennis aujourd'hui?
saloo, tew vuh jooay oh tenees oh-joordwee

Hi, do you want to play tennis today?

Non. Je n'aime pas le sport.
noñ. juh nem pah luh spor

No, I don't like sport.

Alors, quels sont tes intérêts?
alor, kel soñ tay zañtairay

So what are your interests?

4 Useful phrases

Learn these phrases and then test yourself using the cover flap.

What are your (formal/informal) interests?	**Quels sont vos/tes intérêts?** kel soñ voe/tay zañtayray
I like the theatre.	**J'aime le théâtre.** jem luh tay-atruh
I prefer the cinema.	**Je préfère le cinéma.** juh prayfair luh sinaymah
I'm interested in art.	**Je m'intéresse à l'art.** juh mañtairess ah lar
That bores me.	**Ça m'ennuie.** sah moñwee

Je déteste la guitare.
juh daytest lah geetar
I hate guitar music.

la galerie
lah galuree
circle

l'orchestre *(m)*
lorkestruh
stalls

5 Say it

I'm interested in music.

I prefer sport.

I don't like computer games.

Je préfère le shopping.
juh prayfair luh shopping

I prefer shopping.

Ça ne m'intéresse pas.
sah nuh mañtairess pah

That doesn't interest me.

Pas de problème. J'y vais toute seule.
pah de prob-lem. jee vay toot surl

No problem. I'll go on my own.

1 Warm up

Ask "Do you (formal) want to play tennis?" (pp.118–19)

Say "I like the theatre" and "I prefer sightseeing". (pp.118–19)

Say "That doesn't interest me". (pp.118–19)

Le sport et les passe-temps
Sport and hobbies

The verb **faire** (*to do or to make*) is a useful verb for talking about hobbies. **Faire** is followed by **du**, **de la** or **de l'**: **Je fais de la peinture** (*I paint*). You can also use the verb **jouer** (*to play*) when talking about playing sports and music.

2 Words to remember

Memorize these words and then test yourself.

le football/rugby luh futbohl/roogbee	*football/rugby*
le tennis luh tenees	*tennis*
la natation lah natasyoñ	*swimming*
la voile lah vwal	*sailing*
la pêche lah pesh	*fishing*
la peinture lah pañtyur	*painting*
le vélo luh vaylo	*cycling*
la randonnée lah rañdonay	*hiking*

le bunker
luh bañkuh
bunker

le joueur de golf
luh joowur duh golf
golfer

Je joue au golf tout les jours.
juh joo oh golf too lay joor
I play golf every day.

3 Useful phrases

Familiarize yourself with these phrases.

Je fais du rugby. juh fay doo roogbee	*I play rugby.*
Il joue au tennis. eel joo oh tenees	*He plays tennis.*
Elle fait de la peinture. el fay duh lah pañtyur	*She paints.*

4 Faire: to do or to make

The verb **faire** (*to do or to make*) is also used to describe the weather.
Learn its different forms and practise the sample sentences below.

Il fait beau aujourd'hui.
eel fay boe oh-joordwee
It's nice weather today.

le drapeau
luh drapoh
flag

le parcours de golf
luh parkoor duh golf
golf course

I do	**je fais** juh fay
you do (informal)	**tu fais** tew fay
he/she does	**il/elle fait** eel/el fay
we do	**nous faisons** noo fayzon
you do (formal/plural)	**vous faites** voo fet
they do	**ils/elles font** eel/el foñ
I go hiking.	**Je fais de la randonnée.** juh fay duh lah rañdonay
What do you do?	**Que faites-vous?** kuh fet voo
We play tennis.	**Nous faisons du tennis.** noo fayzon doo tenees

5 Put into practice

Practise these phrases. Then cover up the text on the right and
complete the dialogue in French. Check your answers.

Qu'est-ce que vous aimez faire?
keskuh voo zemay fair
What do you like doing?

Say: *I like playing tennis.*

J'aime jouer au tennis.
jem jooway oh tenees

Tu fais du football aussi?
tew fay doo futbohl ohsee
Do you play football as well?

Say: *No. I play rugby.*

Non, je fais du rugby.
noñ, juh fay doo roogbee

🇫🇷 **Cultural tip** France boasts a huge variety
of regional games, such as pelota in the Basque
country. Most popular of all, the French version of
bowls – "pétanque" or "boules" – is played in almost
every town and village.

1 Warm up

Say "my husband"
and "my wife".
(pp.10–11)

How do you say
"lunch" and "dinner"
in French? (pp.20–1)

Say "Sorry, I'm busy".
(pp.32–3)

Voir des gens
Socializing

The French dinner table is the centre
of the social world. You can expect to
do a lot of your socializing enjoying
food and wine. It is best to use the
more polite **vous** form to talk to
people you meet socially until they
call you **tu**, in which case you can
reciprocate.

2 Useful phrases

Learn these phrases and then test yourself.

Je voudrais vous inviter à dîner. juh voodray voo zañveetay ah deenay	*I'd like to invite you for dinner.*
Vous êtes libre mercredi prochain? voo zet leebruh mairkrudee prochen	*Are you free next Wednesday?*
Une autre fois peut-être. oon awtruh fwah putetruh	*Another time perhaps.*

Cultural tip When you go to someone's house
for the first time, it is usual to bring flowers or wine. If
you are invited again having seen your host's house, you
can bring something a little more personal.

3 In conversation

Vous voulez venir dîner mardi?
voo voolay vuneer deenay mardee

Would you like to come to dinner on Tuesday?

Je suis désolée, je suis occupée.
juh swee dayzolay, juh swee zokoopay

I'm sorry, I'm busy.

Pourquoi pas jeudi?
poorkwah pah jurdee

What about Thursday?

4 Words to remember

Familiarize yourself with these words and test yourself using the flap.

l'hôtesse *(f)*
lohtess
hostess

l'invitée *(f)*
lanveetay
guest

party	**la soirée** lah swaray
dinner party	**le dîner** luh deenay
invitation	**l'invitation** lañveetasyoñ
reception	**la réception** lah raysepsyoñ
cocktail party	**le cocktail** luh koktail

5 Put into practice

Join in this conversation.

Vous pouvez venir à une réception ce soir.
voo poovay vuneer ah oon raysepsyoñ suh swah
Can you come to a reception this evening?

Say: Yes, I'd love to.

Oui, avec plaisir.
wee, avek playzeer

Merci de nous avoir invités.
mairsee duh noo zavwar añveetay
Thank you for inviting us.

Ça commence à huit heures.
sah komoñs ah weet ur
It starts at eight o'clock.

Ask: Should I dress formally?

Il faut s'habiller?
eel foe sabeeyay

Avec plaisir.
avek playzeer

With pleasure.

Venez avec votre mari.
vunay avek votruh maree

Please bring your husband.

Merci. A quelle heure?
mairsee. ah kel ur

Thank you. At what time?

Révisez et répétez
Review and repeat

1 Animals

1 **le poisson**
luh pwassoñ

2 **l'oiseau**
lwazoe

3 **le lapin**
luh lapañ

4 **le chat**
luh shah

5 **le hamster**
luh amstair

6 **le chien**
luh shiañ

1 Animals

Say the French words for the numbered animals.

bird ❷

hamster ❺

❶ *fish*

❹ *cat*

2 I like...

1 **J'aime le rugby.**
jem luh roogbee

2 **Je n'aime pas
le golf.**
juh nem pah
luh golf

3 **J'aime faire de
la peinture.**
jem fair duh
lah pañtyur

4 **Je n'aime pas
jouer aux boules.**
juh nem pah
jooway oh bool

2 I like...

Say the following in French.

1 *I like rugby.*

2 *I don't like golf.*

3 *I like painting.*

4 *I don't like playing boules.*

❶

❷

❸

❹

3 rabbit

6 dog

3 To do

Use the correct form of the verb **faire** in these sentences.

1 Tu _____ de la pêche?

2 Elle _____ de la voile.

3 Que _____ vous?

4 Il _____ froid aujourd'hui.

5 Vous _____ de la randonnée?

6 J'aime _____ de la natation.

3 To do

1 **fais**
fay

2 **fait**
fay

3 **faites**
fet

4 **fait**
fay

5 **faites**
fet

6 **faire**
fair

4 An invitation

You are invited for dinner. Join in the conversation, replying in French following the English prompts.

Vous voulez venir pour déjeuner vendredi?
1 *I'm sorry, I'm busy.*

Pourquoi pas samedi?
2 *With pleasure.*

Venez avec vos enfants.
3 *Thank you. At what time?*

A douze heures et demie.
4 *That's good for me.*

4 An invitation

1 **Je suis désolé(e), je suis occupé(e).**
juh swee dayzolay, juh swee zokoopay

2 **Avec plaisir.**
avek playzeer

3 **Merci. A quelle heure?**
mairsee, ah kel ur

4 **C'est bon pour moi.**
say boñ poor mwah

Reinforce and progress

Regular practice is the key to maintaining and advancing your language skills. In this section you will find a variety of suggestions for reinforcing and extending your knowledge of French. Many involve returning to exercises in the book and using the dictionaries to extend their scope. Go back through the lessons in a different order, mix and match activities to make up your own 15-minute daily programme, or focus on topics that are of particular relevance to your current needs.

Keep warmed up

Re-visit the Warm Up boxes to remind yourself of key words and phrases. Make sure you work your way through all of them on a regular basis.

1 Warm up

Say "I'm sorry" (pp.32–3).

What is the French for "I'd like an appointment" (pp.32–3).

How do you say "who?" in French (pp.32–3)?

2 I'd like...

Say you'd like the following:

jam ❷   bread ❸

❶ black coffee

large coffee ❹
with milk

Review and repeat again

Work through a Review and Repeat lesson as a way of reinforcing words and phrases presented in the course. Return to the main lesson for any topic on which you are no longer confident.

3 In conversation: taxi

Carry on conversing

Re-read the In Conversation panels. Say both parts of the conversation, paying attention to the pronunciation. Where possible, try incorporating new words from the dictionary.

Le marché aux fromages, s'il vous plaît.
luh marshayoe fromarj, seel voo play

The cheese market, please.

Oui, sans problème, monsieur.
wee, soñ problem musyuh

Yes, no problem, sir.

Vous pouvez me déposer ici, s'il vou plaît?
voo poovay muh dayposay eesee, see voo play

Can you drop me h please?

4 Useful phrases

Learn these phrases and then test yourself using the flap.

Ouvert	What time do you open/close?	Vous ouvrez/fermez à quelle heure? voo zoovray/fairmay ah kel ur
Toilettes	Where are the toilets?	Où sont les toilettes? oo soh lay twalet
	Is there wheelchair access?	Il y a un accès pour les chaises roulantes? eelyah uñ aksay poor lay shez roolant

Practise phrases

Return to the Useful Phrases and Put into Practice exercises. Test yourself using the cover flap. When you are confident, devise your own versions of the phrases, using new words from the dictionary.

Match, repeat, and extend

Remind yourself of words related to specific topics by returning to the Match and Repeat and Words to Remember exercises. Test yourself using the cover flap. Discover new words in that area by referring to the dictionary and menu guide.

5 Match and repeat

Match the numbered items in this scene with the text in the panel.

1 **les courgettes** (f)
lay korjet

2 **la salade**
lah sal-lad

3 **les citrons** (m)
lay sitroñ

4 **les poireaux** (m)
lay pwaroe

5 **les tomates** (f)
lay toemat

6 **les champignons** (m)
lay shoñpiyoñ

7 **les avocats** (m)
lay zavocah

8 **les pommes de terre** (f)
lay pom duh tair

❷ *lettuce*
❸ *lemons*
❹ *leeks*
❶ *courgettes*
tomatoes ❺
mushrooms ❻
❼ *avocados*
❽ *potatoes*

6 Say it

The lawn needs watering.

Are there any trees?

The gardener comes on Fridays.

Say it again
The Say It exercises are a useful instant reminder for each lesson. Practise these, using your own vocabulary variations from the dictionary or elsewhere in the lesson.

Using other resources

In addition to working with this book, try the following language extension ideas:

● Visit a French-speaking country and try out your new skills with native speakers. Find out if there is a French community near you. There may be shops, cafés, restaurants, and clubs. Try to visit some of these and use your French to order food and drink and strike up conversations. Most native speakers will be happy to speak French to you.

● Join a language class or club. There are usually evening and day classes available at a variety of different levels. Or you could start a club yourself if you have friends who are also interested in keeping up their French.

● Look at French magazines and newspapers. The pictures will help you to understand the text. Advertisements are also a useful way of expanding your vocabulary.

● Use the Internet, where you can find all kinds of websites for learning languages, some of which offer free online help and activities. You can also find French websites for everything from renting a house to shampooing your pet. You can even access French radio and TV stations online. Start by going to a French search engine, such as *voila.fr*, and key a subject that interests you, or set yourself a challenge, for example, finding a two-bedroom house for rent by the sea in Normandy.

Menu guide

This guide lists the most common terms you may encounter on French menus or when shopping for food. If you can't find an exact phrase, try looking up its component parts.

A

abats *offal*
abricot *apricot*
à emporter *to take away*
agneau *lamb*
aiguillette de bœuf *slices of rump steak*
ail *garlic*
ailloli *garlic mayonnaise*
à la broche *spit roast*
à la jardinière *with assorted vegetables*
à la normande *in cream sauce*
à la vapeur *steamed*
amande *almond*
ananas *pineapple*
anchois *anchovies*
andouillette *spicy sausage*
anguille *eel*
à point *medium*
artichaut *artichoke*
asperge *asparagus*
assiette anglaise *selection of cold meats*
au gratin *baked in a milk, cream, and cheese sauce*
au vin blanc *in white wine*
avocat *avocado*

B

banane *banana*
barbue *brill (fish)*
bavaroise *light mousse*
béarnaise *with béarnaise sauce*
bécasse *woodcock*
béchamel *white sauce*
beignet *fritter, doughnut*
beignet aux pommes *apple fritter*
betterave *beetroot*
beurre *butter*
beurre d'anchois *anchovy paste*
beurre noir *dark, melted butter*
bien cuit *well done*
bière *beer*
bière à la pression *draught beer*
bière blonde *lager*
bière brune *bitter beer*
bière panachée *shandy*
bifteck *steak*
bisque d'écrevisses *crayfish soup*

bisque de homard *lobster soup*
biscuit de Savoie *sponge cake*
blanquette de veau *veal stew*
bleu *very rare*
bleu d'auvergne *blue cheese from Auvergne*
bœuf bourguignon *beef cooked in red wine*
bœuf braisé *braised beef*
bœuf en daube *beef casserole*
bœuf miroton *beef and onion stew*
bœuf mode *beef stew with carrots*
bolet *boletus (mushroom)*
boudin blanc *white pudding*
boudin noir *black pudding*
bouillabaisse *fish soup*
bouilli *boiled*
bouillon *broth*
bouillon de légumes *vegetable stock*
bouillon de poule *chicken stock*
boulette *meatball*
bouquet rose *prawns*
bourride *fish soup*
brandade *cod in cream and garlic*
brioche *round roll*
brochet *pike*
brochette *kebab*
brugnon *nectarine*
brûlot *flambéed brandy*
brut *very dry*

C

cabillaud *cod*
café *coffee (black)*
café au lait *white coffee*
café complet *continental breakfast*
café crème *white coffee*
café glacé *iced coffee*
café liégeois *iced coffee with cream*
caille *quail*
calamar/calmar *squid*
calvados *apple brandy*
canapé *small open sandwich, canapé*
canard *duck*
canard laqué *Peking duck*

caneton *duckling*
cantal *white cheese from Auvergne*
câpres *capers*
carbonnade *beef cooked in beer*
cari *curry*
carotte *carrot*
carottes Vichy *carrots in butter and parsley*
carpe *carp*
carré d'agneau *rack of lamb*
carrelet *plaice*
carte *menu*
carte des vins *wine list*
casse-croûte *snacks*
cassis *blackcurrant*
cassoulet *bean, pork and duck casserole*
céleri/céleri rave *celeriac*
céleri en branches *celery*
cèpe *cep (mushroom)*
cerise *cherry*
cerises à l'eau de vie *cherries in brandy*
cervelle *brains*
chabichou *goat's and cow's milk cheese*
chablis *dry white wine from Burgundy*
champignon *mushroom*
champignon de Paris *white button mushroom*
chantilly *whipped cream*
charcuterie *sausages, ham and pâtés; pork products*
charlotte *dessert with fruit, cream, and biscuits*
chausson aux pommes *apple turnover*
cheval *horse*
chèvre *goat's cheese*
chevreuil *venison*
chicorée *endive*
chocolat chaud *hot chocolate*
chocolat glacé *iced chocolate*
chou *cabbage*
chou à la crème *cream puff*
choucroute *sauerkraut with sausages and ham*
chou-fleur *cauliflower*
chou rouge *red cabbage*
choux de Bruxelles *Brussels sprouts*

cidre *cider*
cidre doux *sweet cider*
citron *lemon*
citron pressé *fresh lemon juice*
civet de lièvre *jugged hare*
clafoutis *baked batter pudding with fruit*
cochon de lait *suckling pig*
cocktail de crevettes *prawn cocktail*
cœur *heart*
coing *quince*
colin *hake*
compote *stewed fruit*
comté *hard cheese from the Jura*
concombre *cucumber*
confit de canard *duck preserved in fat*
confit d'oie *goose preserved in fat*
confiture *jam*
congre *conger eel*
consommé *clear meat or chicken soup*
coq au vin *chicken in red wine*
coque *cockle*
coquelet *cockerel*
coquilles Saint-Jacques *scallops in cream sauce*
côte de porc *pork chop*
côtelette *chop*
cotriade bretonne *fish soup from Brittany*
coulommiers *rich, soft cheese*
court-bouillon *stock*
crabe *crab*
crème *cream; creamy sauce or dessert; white (coffee)*
crème à la vanille *vanilla custard*
crème anglaise *custard*
crème chantilly *whipped cream*
crème d'asperges *cream of asparagus soup*
crème de bolets *cream of mushroom soup*
crème de volaille *cream of chicken soup*
crème d'huîtres *cream of oyster soup*
crème fouettée *whipped cream*
crème pâtissière *rich, creamy custard*
crème renversée *set custard*
crème vichyssoise *cold leek and potato soup*
crêpe *pancake*
crêpe à la crème de marron *pancake with chestnut cream*
crêpe à l'œuf *pancake with fried egg*

crêpe de froment *wheat pancake*
crêpes Suzette *pancakes flambéed with orange sauce*
crépinette *small sausage patty wrapped in fat*
cresson *cress*
crevette grise *shrimp*
crevette rose *prawn*
croque-madame *grilled cheese and ham sandwich with a fried egg*
croque-monsieur *grilled cheese and ham sandwich*
crottin de Chavignol *small goat's cheese*
crustacés *shellfish*
cuisses de grenouille *frogs' legs*

D

dartois *pastry with jam*
dégustation *wine tasting*
digestif *liqueur*
dinde *turkey*
doux *sweet*

E

eau minérale gazeuse *sparkling mineral water*
eau minérale plate *still mineral water*
échalote *shallot*
écrevisse *freshwater crayfish*
endive *chicory*
en papillote *baked in foil or paper*
entrecôte *rib steak*
entrecôte au poivre *peppered rib steak*
entrecôte maître d'hôtel *steak with butter and parsley*
entrée *starter*
entremets *dessert*
épaule d'agneau farcie *stuffed shoulder of lamb*
épinards en branches *leaf spinach*
escalope de veau milanaise *veal escalope with tomato sauce*
escalope panée *breaded escalope*
escargot *snail*
estouffade de bœuf *beef casserole*
estragon *tarragon*

F

faisan *pheasant*
farci *stuffed*
fenouil *fennel*
filet *fillet*
filet de bœuf Rossini *fillet of beef with foie gras*

filet de perche *perch fillet*
fine *fine brandy*
flageolets *kidney beans*
flan *custard tart*
foie de veau *veal liver*
foie gras *goose or duck liver preserve*
foies de volaille *chicken livers*
fonds d'artichaut *artichoke hearts*
fondue bourguignonne *meat fondue*
fondue savoyarde *cheese fondue*
fraise *strawberry*
fraise des bois *wild strawberry*
framboise *raspberry*
frisée *curly lettuce*
frit *deep-fried*
frites *chips*
fromage *cheese*
fromage blanc *cream cheese*
fromage de chèvre *goat's cheese*
fruits de mer *seafood*

G

galette *round, flat cake or savoury wholemeal crêpe*
garni *with potatoes and vegetables*
gâteau *cake*
gaufre *wafer; waffle*
gelée *jelly*
Gewürztraminer *dry white wine from Alsace*
gibier *game*
gigot d'agneau *leg of lamb*
girolle *chanterelle (mushroom)*
glace *ice cream*
goujon *gudgeon (fish)*
gratin *dish baked with milk, cheese, and cream*
gratin dauphinois *sliced potatoes baked in milk, cream, and cheese*
gratinée *baked onion soup*
grillé *grilled*
grondin *gurnard (fish)*
groseille rouge *redcurrant*

H

hachis parmentier *shepherd's pie*
hareng mariné *marinated herring*
haricots *beans*
haricots blancs *haricot beans*
haricots verts *green beans*
homard *lobster*
hors-d'œuvre *starter*
huître *oyster*

I, J

îles flottantes *floating islands* (soft meringue on custard)
infusion *herb tea*
jambon *ham*
jambon de Bayonne *smoked and cured ham*
julienne *soup with chopped vegetables*
jus de fruits *fruit juice*
jus de pomme *apple juice*
jus d'orange *orange juice*

K, L

kir *white wine with blackcurrant liqueur*
kirsch *cherry brandy*
lait *milk*
laitue *lettuce*
langouste *saltwater crayfish*
langoustine *Dublin Bay prawn*
lapereau *young rabbit*
lapin *rabbit*
lapin de garenne *wild rabbit*
lard *bacon*
légume *vegetable*
lentilles *lentils*
lièvre *hare*
limande *lemon sole*
livarot *strong, soft cheese from the north of France*
longe *loin*
lotte *monkfish*
loup au fenouil *bass with fennel*

M

macédoine de légumes *mixed vegetables*
mache *corn salad* (leafy vegetable)
mangue *mango*
maquereau *mackerel*
marc *grape brandy*
marcassin *young boar*
marchand de vin *in red wine sauce*
marron *chestnut*
massepain *marzipan*
menthe *peppermint*
menthe à l'eau *mint cordial with water*
menu du jour *today's menu*
menu gastronomique *gourmet menu*
menu touristique *tourist menu*
merlan *whiting*
millefeuille *custard slice*
millésime *vintage*
morille *morel* (mushroom)
morue *cod*

moules *mussels*
moules marinière *mussels in white wine*
mousseux *sparkling*
moutarde *mustard*
mouton *mutton*
mulet *mullet*
munster *strong cheese*
mûre *blackberry*
Muscadet *dry white wine*
myrtille *bilberry*

N

nature *plain*
navarin *mutton stew with vegetables*
navet *turnip*
noisette *hazelnut*
noisette d'agneau *medallion of lamb*
noix *nuts, walnuts*
nouilles *noodles*

O

œuf à la coque *boiled egg*
œuf dur *hard-boiled egg*
œuf mollet *soft-boiled egg*
œuf poché *poached egg*
œufs brouillés *scrambled eggs*
œuf sur le plat *fried egg*
oie *goose*
oignon *onion*
omelette au naturel *plain omelette*
omelette aux fines herbes *herb omelette*
omelette paysanne *omelette with potatoes and bacon*
orange pressée *fresh orange juice*
oseille *sorrel*
oursin *sea urchin*

P

pain *bread*
pain au chocolat *chocolate croissant*
palette de porc *shoulder of pork*
palourde *clam*
pamplemousse *grapefruit*
pastis *anise-flavoured alcoholic drink*
pâté de canard *duck pâté*
pâté de foie de volaille *chicken liver pâté*
pâte feuilletée *puff pastry*
pâtes *pasta*
pêche *peach*
perdreau *young partridge*
perdrix *partridge*
petite friture *whitebait*
petit pain *roll*
petit pois *peas*
petits fours *small pastries*

petit suisse *cream cheese*
pied de porc *pig's feet*
pigeonneau *young pigeon*
pignatelle *cheese fritter*
pilaf de mouton *rice dish with mutton*
pintade *guinea fowl*
piperade *dish of egg, tomatoes, and peppers*
pissaladière *Provençal dish similar to pizza*
pistache *pistachio*
plat du jour *dish of the day*
plateau de fromages *cheese board*
pochouse *fish casserole with white wine*
poire *pear*
poireau *leek*
poisson *fish*
poivre *pepper*
poivron *red/green pepper*
pomme *apple*
pomme de terre *potato*
pommes de terre à l'anglaise *boiled potatoes*
pommes de terre en robe de chambre/des champs *baked potatoes*
pommes de terre sautées *fried potatoes*
pommes frites *chips*
pommes paille *finely cut chips*
pommes vapeur *steamed potatoes*
porc *pork*
potage *soup*
potage bilibi *fish and oyster soup*
potage Crécy *carrot and rice soup*
potage cressonnière *watercress soup*
potage Esaü *lentil soup*
potage parmentier *leek and potato soup*
potage printanier *vegetable soup*
potage Saint-Germain *split pea soup*
potage velouté *creamy soup*
pot-au-feu *beef and vegetable stew*
potée *vegetable and meat stew*
Pouilly-Fuissé *dry white wine from Burgundy*
poule au pot *chicken and vegetable stew*
poulet basquaise *chicken with ratatouille*
poulet chasseur *chicken with mushrooms and white wine*
poulet créole *chicken in white sauce with rice*
poulet rôti *roast chicken*
praire *clam*

provençale *with tomatoes, garlic and herbs*
prune *plum*
pruneau *prune*
pudding *plum pudding*
purée *mashed potatoes*

Q

quenelle *meat or fish dumpling*
queue de bœuf *oxtail*
quiche lorraine *egg, bacon, and cream tart*

R

raclette *Swiss dish of melted cheese*
radis *radish*
ragoût *stew*
raie *skate*
raie au beurre noir *skate fried in butter*
raifort *horseradish*
raisin *grape*
râpé *grated*
rascasse *scorpion fish*
ratatouille *stew of peppers, courgettes, aubergines, and tomatoes*
ravigote *herb dressing*
reblochon *strong cheese from Savoy*
rémoulade *mayonnaise dressing with herbs, mustard, and capers*
rigotte *small goat's cheese from Lyon*
rillettes *potted pork or goose meat*
ris de veau *veal sweetbread*
riz *rice*
riz pilaf *spicy rice with meat or seafood*
rognon *kidney*
roquefort *blue cheese*
rôti *roasted/joint of meat*
rouget *mullet*

S

sabayon *zabaglione (whipped egg yolk in Marsala wine)*
sablé *shortbread*
saignant *rare*
saint-honoré *cream puff cake*
saint-marcellin *goat's cheese*
salade composée *mixed salad*
salade russe *diced vegetables in mayonnaise*
salade verte *green salad*
salmis *game stew*
salsifis *oyster plant, salsify*
sanglier *wild boar*

sauce aurore *white sauce with tomato purée*
sauce béarnaise *thick sauce of eggs and butter*
sauce blanche *white sauce*
sauce gribiche *dressing with hard-boiled eggs*
sauce hollandaise *rich sauce of eggs, butter and vinegar, served with fish*
sauce Madère *Madeira sauce*
sauce matelote *wine sauce*
sauce Mornay *béchamel sauce with cheese*
sauce mousseline *hollandaise sauce with cream*
sauce poulette *sauce of mushrooms and egg yolks*
sauce ravigote *dressing with shallots and herbs*
sauce suprême *creamy sauce*
sauce tartare *mayonnaise with herbs and gherkins*
sauce veloutée *white sauce with egg yolks and cream*
sauce vinot *wine sauce*
saucisse *sausage*
saucisse de Francfort *frankfurter*
saucisse de Strasbourg *beef sausage*
saucisson *salami*
saumon *salmon*
saumon fumé *smoked salmon*
sauternes *sweet white wine*
savarin *rum baba*
sec *dry*
seiche *cuttlefish*
sel *salt*
service (non) compris *service (not) included*
service 12% inclus *12% service charge included*
sole bonne femme *sole in white wine and mushrooms*
sole meunière *floured sole fried in butter*
soupe *soup*
soupe au pistou *thick vegetable soup with basil*
steak au poivre *peppered steak*
steak frites *steak and chips*
steak haché *minced meat, minced beef*
steak tartare *raw minced beef with a raw egg*
sucre *sugar*
suprême de volaille *chicken in cream sauce*

T

tanche *tench (fish)*
tarte aux fraises *strawberry tart*
tarte aux pommes *apple tart*
tarte frangipane *almond cream tart*
tartelette *small tart*
tarte Tatin *baked apple dish*
tartine *bread and butter*
tendrons de veau *breast of veal*
terrine *pâté*
tête de veau *calf's head*
thé *tea*
thé à la menthe *mint tea*
thé au lait *tea with milk*
thé citron *lemon tea*
thon *tuna*
tomates farcies *stuffed tomatoes*
tome de Savoie *white cheese from Savoy*
tournedos *round beef steak*
tourte *covered pie*
tourteau *type of crab*
tripes à la mode de Caen *tripe in spicy vegetable sauce*
truite au bleu *poached trout*
truite aux amandes *trout with almonds*
truite meunière *trout in flour and fried in butter*

V, Y

vacherin *strong, soft cheese from the Jura*
vacherin glacé *ice cream meringue*
veau *veal*
velouté de tomate *cream of tomato soup*
vermicelle *vermicelli (very fine pasta)*
viande *meat*
vin *wine*
vinaigrette *French dressing*
vin blanc *white wine*
vin de pays *local wine*
vin de table *table wine*
vin rosé *rosé wine*
vin rouge *red wine*
volaille *poultry*
VSOP *mature brandy*
yaourt *yoghurt*

Dictionary
English to French

The gender of a singular French noun is indicated by the word for *the*: **le** and **la** (masculine and feminine). If these are abbreviated to **l'** in front of a vowel or the letter "h", or if the noun is plural, indicated by **les**, then the gender is indicated by the abbreviations "(m)" or "(f)". French adjectives (adj) vary according to the gender and number of the word they describe; the masculine form is shown here. In most cases, you add an **-e** to the masculine form to make it feminine. Certain endings use a different rule: masculine adjectives that end in **-x** adopt an **-se** ending in the feminine form, while those that end in **-ien** change to **-ienne**. Some feminine adjectives that do not follow these rules are shown here and follow the abbreviation "(fem)". For the plural form, a (silent) **-s** is usually added.

A

a un/une
about: about sixteen environ seize
accelerator l'accélérateur (m)
accident l'accident (m)
accommodation l'hébergement (m)
accountant le/la comptable
ache la douleur
adaptor (plug) la prise multiple; (voltage) l'adaptateur (m)
address l'adresse (f)
adhesive l'adhésif (m)
admission charge le prix d'entrée
advance l'avance (f)
after après
afternoon l'après-midi (m)
aftershave l'après-rasage (m)
again de nouveau
against contre
agenda l'ordre du jour (m)
agent l'agent (m)
AIDS SIDA
air l'air (m)
air conditioning la climatisation
aircraft l'avion (m)
airline la compagnie aérienne
air mail par avion
air mattress le matelas pneumatique
airport l'aéroport (m)

airport bus la navette (pour l'aéroport)
aisle (supermarket) rayon
alarm clock le réveil
alcohol l'alcool (m)
Algeria l'Algérie (f)
Algerian algérien(ne)
all tout; *all the streets* toutes les rues; *that's all* c'est tout
allergic allergique
almost presque
alone seul
Alps les Alpes (f)
already déjà
always toujours
am: I am je suis
ambulance l'ambulance (f)
America l'Amérique (f)
American américain(e)
and et
Andorra Andorre
ankle la cheville
another (different) un/une autre; *another coffee, please* encore un café, s'il vous plaît
answering machine le répondeur
antifreeze l'antigel (m)
antique shop le magasin d'antiquités; l'antiquaire (m)
antiseptic l'antiseptique (m)
apartment l'appartement (m)
aperitif l'apéritif (m)
appetite l'appétit (m)
apple la pomme

application form le formulaire de demande
appointment le rendez-vous
apricot l'abricot (m)
April avril
architecture l'architecture (f)
are: you are (singular informal) tu es; *we are* nous sommes; (plural; singular formal) vous êtes; *they are* ils/elles sont
arm le bras
armchair le fauteuil
arrival l'arrivée (f)
arrive arriver
art l'art (m)
art gallery le musée d'art; la galerie d'art
artist l'artiste (m)
as: as soon as possible dès que possible
ashtray le cendrier
asleep endormi; *he's asleep* il dort
aspirin l'aspirine (f)
asthmatic asthmatique
at: at the post office à la poste; *at the café* au café; *at 3 o'clock* à 3 heures
attic le grenier
attractive attirant
August août
aunt la tante
Australia l'Australie (f)
Australian australien(ne)
automatic automatique
autumn l'automne (m)

avocado l'avocat (m)

away: is it far away?
est-ce que c'est loin?;
go away! allez-vous
en!

awful affreux

axe la hache

axle l'essieu (m)

B

baby le bébé

baby wipes
les lingettes (f)

back (not front)
l'arrière (m); *(body)*
le dos; *I'll come back
tomorrow* je reviendrai
demain

backpack le sac à dos

bacon le bacon;
bacon and eggs
des œufs au bacon

bad mauvais

baggage
les bagages (m)

baggage check in
l'enregistrement des
bagages (m)

baggage claim la
réclamation de
bagages

bait l'appât (m)

bake cuire

bakery la boulangerie

balcony le balcon

bald chauve

ball (football etc) le
ballon; *(tennis etc)*
la balle

ballpoint pen le stylo-
bille

banana la banane

band (musicians) le
groupe

bandage le pansement,
le bandage

bank la banque

banknote le billet

bar le bar

barbecue le barbecue

barber's le coiffeur

bargain la affaire

basement le sous-sol

basin (sink) le lavabo

basket le panier

bath le bain;
(bathtub) la
baignoire; *to have a
bath* prendre un bain

bathroom la salle de
bains

battery (car) la batterie;
(torch) la pile

be être

beach la plage

beans les haricots (m)

beard la barbe

beautiful beau, *(fem)*
belle

because parce que

bed le lit

bed linen
les draps (m)

bedroom la chambre

beef le bœuf

beer la bière

before avant

beginner le débutant,
la débutante

beginners' slope la piste
pour débutants

behind derrière

beige beige

Belgian belge

Belgium la Belgique

bell (church) la cloche;
(door) la sonnette

below ... sous ...

belt la ceinture

beside à côté de

best: the best
le meilleur

better mieux

between ... entre ...

bicycle la bicyclette,
le vélo

big grand

bill l'addition (f)

bin liner
le sac poubelle

bird l'oiseau (m)

birthday
l'anniversaire (m);
happy birthday!
joyeux anniversaire!

biscuit le biscuit

bite (by dog) la
morsure; *(by snake)*
la piqûre, *(verb: dog)*
insect; mordre;
(insect, snake)
piquer

bitter amer

black noir

blackberry la mûre

blackcurrant le cassis

blanket la couverture

bleach l'eau de Javel
(f); *(verb)* décolorer

blind (cannot see)
aveugle; *(window)*
le store

blister l'ampoule (f)

blizzard la tempête
de neige

blond (adj) blond

blood le sang

blood test la prise de
sang

blouse le chemisier

blue bleu

boarding pass la carte
d'embarquement

boat le bateau;
(smaller) la barque

body le corps

boil (verb) bouillir

boiled bouilli

boiler le chauffe-eau

bolt (on door) le
verrou; verrouiller
(verb)

bone l'os (m); *(fish)*
l'arête (f)

bonnet (car) le capot

book le livre; réserver
(verb)

bookshop la librairie

boot (footwear) la
botte; *(car)* le coffre

border la frontière

boring ennuyeux

born: I was born in ...
je suis né(e) en ...

both les deux; *both
of them* tous les deux;
both of us nous deux;
both large and small
grand et petit à la fois

bottle la bouteille

bottle opener le
décapsuleur, l'ouvre-
bouteille (m)

*bottom: le fond;
(part of body)*
le derrière

bowl le bol; *(animal)*
la gamelle

box la boîte

box office (theatre etc)
le bureau de location

boy le garçon

boyfriend le petit ami

bra le soutien-gorge

bracelet le bracelet

braces (clothes) les
bretelles (f)

brake le frein; freiner
(verb)

branch la branche

brandy le cognac

bread le pain

breakdown (car) la
panne; *(nervous)*
la dépression; *I've
had a breakdown
(car)* je suis tombé
en panne

breakfast le petit
déjeuner

breathe respirer

bricklayer le maçon

bridge le pont

briefcase
l'attaché-case (m)

British britannique

Brittany la Bretagne

brochure la brochure

broken cassé; *broken
leg* la jambe cassée;
broken down en
panne

brooch la broche

brother le frère

brown marron

bruise le bleu

brush la brosse;
(paintbrush) le
pinceau; *(broom)* le
balai; *(verb)* brosser

Brussels Bruxelles

bucket le seau

budget le budget

(verb) boire; *would you like a drink?* vous voulez boire quelque chose?

drinking water l'eau potable (f)

drive (verb: car) conduire

driver le conducteur

driveway le passage

driving licence le permis de conduire

drops les goutes (f)

drunk soûl, ivre

dry sec, (fem) sèche

dry cleaner's le pressing

during pendant

duster le chiffon à poussière

duty-free hors-taxe

duvet la couette

E

each (every) chaque; *two euros each* deux euros pièce

ear l'oreille (f)

early tôt

earrings les boucles d'oreille (f)

east l'est (m)

easy facile

eat manger

egg l'œuf (m)

eight huit

eighteen dix-huit

eighty quatre-vingt

either: either of them n'importe lequel; *either ... or ...* soit ... soit ...

elastic élastique

elastic band l'élastique (m)

elbow le coude

electric électrique

electrician électricien(ne)

electricity l'électricité (f)

eleven onze

else: something else autre chose; *someone else* quelqu'un d'autre; *somewhere else* ailleurs

e-mail l'email (m), le message, la messagerie électronique

e-mail address l'adresse électronique (f)

embarrassing gênant

embassy l'ambassade (f)

embroidery la broderie

emerald l'émeraude (f)

emergency l'urgence (f)

emergency departement la salle des urgences

emergency exit la sortie de secours

empty vide

end la fin

engaged (couple) fiancé

engine (car) le moteur; (train) la locomotive

engineer l'ingénieur (m)

engineering l'ingénierie (f)

England l'Angleterre (f)

English anglais(e)

enlargement l'agrandissement (m)

enough assez

entertainment le divertissement

entrance l'entrée (f)

envelope l'enveloppe (f)

epileptic épileptique

eraser la gomme

escalator l'escalier roulant (m)

especially particulièrement

estimate l'estimation (f)

evening le soir

every chaque

everyone tout le monde

everything tout

everywhere partout

example l'exemple (m); *for example* par exemple

excellent excellent

excess baggage l'excédent de bagages (m)

exchange (verb) échanger

exchange rate le taux de change

excursion l'excursion (f)

excuse me! pardon!

executive (in company) cadre (m)

exhaust (car) le pot d'échappement

exhibition l'exposition (f)

exit la sortie

expensive cher

extension lead la rallonge

exterior l'extérieure (m); extérieure (adj)

eye l'œil (m)

eyebrow le sourcil

eyes les yeux (m)

F

face le visage

faint vague; *to faint* evanouir

fair la foire; (just) juste; *it's not fair* ce n'est pas juste

fan (ventilator) le ventilateur; (enthusiast) le/la fan

fan belt la courroie du ventilateur

fantastic fantastique

far loin; *how far is it to ...?* est-ce que ... est loin d'ici?

fare le prix du billet

farm la ferme

farmer le fermier

fashion la mode

fast rapide

fat (of person) gros, (fem) grosse; (on meat etc) le gras

father le père

fax le fax; (verb: document) faxer

fax machine le fax

February fevrier

feel (touch) toucher; *I feel hot* j'ai chaud; *I feel like ...* j'ai envie de ...; *I don't feel well* je ne me sens pas bien

feet les pieds (m)

felt-tip pen le feutre

ferry (small) le bac; (large) le ferry

fever la fièvre

fiancé le fiancé

fiancée la fiancée

field le champ; (academic) secteur (m)

fifteen quinze

fifty cinquante

fig la figue

figures les chiffres (m)

filling (in tooth) le plombage; (in sandwich, cake) la garniture

film le film

filter paper le papier filtre

finger le doigt

fire le feu; (blaze) l'incendie (m)

fire extinguisher l'extincteur (m)

fireplace la cheminée

fireworks le feu d'artifice

first premier

first aid les premiers soins (m)

first class première classe

first floor le premier étage

first name le prénom
fish le poisson
fishing la pêche;
  to go fishing aller à
  la pêche
fishing rod la canne à
  pêche
fishmonger's la
  poissonnerie
five cinq
fizzy water l'eau
  gazeuse (f)
flag le drapeau
flash (camera)
  le flash
flat (level) plat
flat tyre le pneu crevé
flavour le goût
flea la puce
flight le vol
flight attendant
  l'hôtesse de l'air (f)
flip-flops les tongs (f)
flippers les palmes (f)
floor (ground) le
  plancher; (storey)
  l'étage (m)
florist la fleuriste
flour la farine
flower la fleur
flowerbed le parterre
  de fleurs
flute la flûte
fly (insect) la mouche;
  (verb: of plane etc)
  voler; (of person)
  prendre l'avion
fog le brouillard
folk music la musique
  folklorique
food la nourriture
food poisoning
  l'intoxication
  alimentaire (f)
foot le pied
football le football
for pour; *for me* pour
  moi; *what for?* pour
  quoi faire?; *for a
  week* pour une
  semaine
foreigner
  l'étranger (m)
forest la forêt
forget oublier
fork la fourchette
fortnight quinze jours
forty quarante
fountain pen le stylo-
  plume
four quatre
fourteen quatorze
fourth quatrième
France la France
free (no cost) gratuit;
  (at liberty) libre
freezer le congélateur
French français(e)
Friday vendredi
fridge le frigo
fried frit

friend l'ami(e)
friendly amical, gentil
fringe la frange
front: in front devant
frost le gel
frozen foods les produits
  surgelés (m)
fruit le fruit
fruit juice le jus de fruit
fry frire
frying pan la poêle
full complet; *I'm full!*
  j'ai l'estomac bien
  rempli!
full board la pension
  complète
funny drôle
furnished meublé
furniture
  les meubles (m)

G

garage le garage
garden le jardin
garden centre la
  jardinerie
garlic l'ail (m)
gas le gaz
gas-permeable lenses
  les lentilles semi-
  souples (f)
gate le portail, la grille;
  (at airport) la porte
  d'embarquement
gay homosexuel
gear (car) la vitesse
gearbox la boîte de
  vitesses
gearstick le levier de
  vitesse
gel le gel
German allemand(e)
Germany
  l'Allemagne (f)
get (fetch) aller
  chercher; *have you
  got …?* avez-vous …?;
  to get the train
  prendre le train;
  *get back: we get
  back tomorrow* nous
  rentrons demain;
  *to get something
  back* récupérer
  quelque chose
get in entrer; (arrive)
  arriver
get off (bus etc)
  descendre
get on (bus etc) monter
get out sortir
get up se lever
gift le cadeau
gin le gin
ginger le gingembre
girl (child) la fille;
  (young woman)
  la jeune fille
girlfriend
  la petite amie

give donner
glad heureux
glass le verre
glasses
  les lunettes (f)
gloves les gants (m)
glue la colle
go aller
gold l'or (m)
golf le golf
golf course le parcours
  de golf
good bon, (fem) bonne;
  good! bien!
goodbye au revoir
good evening bonsoir
government le
  gouvernement
granddaughter la
  petite-fille
grandfather
  le grand-père
grandmother
  la grand-mère
grandparents les
  grands-parents (m)
grandson le petit-fils
grapes les raisins (m)
grass l'herbe (f)
Great Britain
  la Grande-Bretagne
green vert
grey gris
grill le gril
grilled grillé(e)
grocer's l'épicerie (f)
ground floor
  le rez-de-chaussée
groundsheet le tapis
  de sol
guarantee la garantie;
  (verb) garantir
guard (train) le chef
  de train
guest l'invitée
guide le/la guide
guide book le guide
guitar la guitare
gun (rifle) le fusil;
  (pistol) le pistolet
gutter la gouttière

H

hair les cheveux (m);
  long/short hair les
  cheveux longs/
  courts
haircut la coupe (de
  cheveux)
hairdresser le coiffeur
hairdryer le sèche-
  cheveux
hairspray la laque
half demi; *half an
  hour* une demi-heure
half board la demi-
  pension
ham le jambon
hamburger le
  hamburger

hammer le marteau
hamster le hamster
hand la main
hand luggage le bagage à main
handbag le sac à main
handbrake le frein à main
handkerchief le mouchoir
handle (door) la poignée
handsome beau
hangover la gueule de bois
happy heureux
harbour le port
hard dur; (difficult) difficile
hard lenses les lentilles rigides (f)
hardware shop la quincaillerie
hat le chapeau
have avoir; *have you got …?* avez-vous …?
hay fever le rhume des foins
he il
head la tête
head office le siège social
headache le mal à la tête
headlights les phares (m)
headphones les écouteurs (m)
hear entendre
hearing aid l'appareil acoustique
heart le cœur
heart condition le problème au cœur
hearts (cards) cœurs
heater le radiateur
heating le chauffage
heavy lourd
hedge la haie
heel le talon
hello bonjour
help l'aide (f); (verb) aider
hepatitis l'hépatite (f)
her: it's for her c'est pour elle; *give it to her* donnez-le lui
her: her book son livre; *her house* sa maison; *her shoes* ses chaussures; *it's hers* c'est à elle
hi salut
high haut
highway code le code de la route
hiking la randonée
hill la colline
him: it's for him c'est pour lui; *give it to him* donnez-le lui

his: his book son livre; *his house* sa maison; *his shoes* ses chaussures; *it's his* c'est à lui
history l'histoire (f)
hitchhike faire de l'autostop
HIV positive séropositif(ve)
hobby le passe-temps
holiday les vacances (f)
home: at home (my home) chez moi; *he's at home* il est chez lui
homeopathy homéopathie
honest honnête
honey le miel
honeymoon la lune de miel
horn (car) le klaxon; (animal) la corne
horrible horrible
hospital l'hôpital (m)
host l'hôte (m)
hostess l'hôtesse (f)
hot chaud
hotel l'hôtel (m)
hour l'heure (f)
house la maison
household products les produits entretien (m)
hovercraft l'aéroglisseur (m)
hoverport l'hoverport (m)
how? comment?
how much? combien?
hundred cent
hungry: I'm hungry j'ai faim
hurry: I'm in a hurry je suis pressé
husband le mari
hydrofoil l'hydrofoil (m)

I

I je
ice la glace
ice cream la glace
ice rink la patinoire
ice skates les patins à glace (m)
ice-skating: to go ice-skating aller patiner
identification identification
if si
ignition l'allumage (m)
ill malade
immediately immédiatement
impossible impossible
in dans; *in France* en France
indicator le clignotant
indigestion l'indigestion (f)

inexpensive bon marché, pas cher
infection l'infection (f)
information l'information (f)
injection la piqûre
injury la blessure
ink l'encre (f)
inn l'auberge (f)
inner tube la chambre à air
insect l'insecte (m)
insect repellent la crème anti-insecte
insomnia l'insomnie (f)
instant coffee le café soluble
insurance l'assurance (f)
interesting intéressant
internet l'internet (m)
interpret interpréter
interpreter l'interprète (m)
invitation l'invitation (f)
invoice la facture
Ireland l'Irlande (f)
Irish irlandais(e)
iron ((for clothes) le fer à repasser; (verb) repasser
is: he/she is il/elle est; *it is* c'est
island l'île (f)
it il; elle
Italian italien(ne)
Italy l'Italie (f)
its son; sa; ses (see his)

J

jacket la veste
jam la confiture
January janvier
jazz le jazz
jeans les jeans (m)
jellyfish la méduse
jeweller's la bijouterie
job le travail
jog (verb) faire du jogging; *to go for a jog* aller faire du jogging
joke la plaisanterie
journey le voyage
July juillet
June juin
just: it's just arrived ça vient juste d'arriver; *I've just one left* il ne m'en reste qu'un

K

kettle la bouilloire
key la clé
keyboard le clavier
kidney le rein
kilo le kilo
kilometre le kilomètre
kind gentil
kitchen la cuisine

knee le genou
knife le couteau
knit tricoter
knitting needle l'aiguille à tricoter (f)
know (fact) savoir; (person) connaître; *I don't know* je ne sais pas

L

label l'étiquette (f)
lace la dentelle; (of shoe) le lacet
lake le lac
lamb l'agneau (m)
lamp la lampe
lampshade l'abat-jour (m)
land la terre; (verb) atterrir
language la langue
laptop l'ordinateur portable (m)
large grand
last (final) dernier; *last week* la semaine dernière; *at last!* enfin!
late tard; *the bus is late* le bus est en retard
later plus tard
laugh rire
launderette la laverie automatique
laundry (place) la blanchisserie; (clothes) le linge
law (subject) le droit
lawn la pelouse
lawn mower la tondeuse à gazon
lawyer avocat(e)
laxative le laxatif
lazy paresseux
lead la laisse
leaf la feuille
leaflet le dépliant
learn apprendre
leather le cuir
lecture theatre l'amphithéâtre (m)
leek le poireaux
left (not right) la gauche; *there's nothing left* il ne reste plus rien
leg la jambe
lemon le citron
lemonade la limonade
length la longueur
lens (camera) l'objectif (m)
less moins
lesson la leçon
letter la lettre
lettuce la salade
library la bibliothèque
licence le permis
life la vie
lift l'ascenseur (m)

light la lumière; (not heavy) léger; (not dark) clair
light bulb l'ampoule (f)
lighter le briquet
lighter fluid le gaz à briquet
light meter la cellule photoélectrique
like (verb) aimer: *I like swimming* j'aime nager; *I don't like* je n'aime pas; (similar to) comme
lime (fruit) le citron vert
lipstick le rouge à lèvres
liqueur la liqueur
list la liste
literature la litérature
litre le litre
litter les ordures (f)
little (small) petit; *it's a little big* c'est un peu trop grand; *just a little* juste un peu
liver le foie
living room le salon
lobster le homard
lollipop la sucette
long long, (fem) longue
lost property les objets trouvés (m)
loud fort; (colour) criard
love l'amour (m); (verb) aimer
lover l'amant (m)
low bas
luck la chance; *good luck!* bonne chance!
luggage les bagages (m)
luggage lockers la consigne automatique
luggage rack le porte-bagages
lunch le déjeuner
Luxembourg le Luxembourg

M

mad fou, (fem) folle
magazine la revue
maid la femme de chambre
main courses les plats (m)
make faire
make-up le maquillage
man l'homme (m)
manager le directeur; le chef
many beaucoup; *not many* pas beaucoup
map la carte; (town map) le plan
March mars
margarine la margarine
market le marché

marmalade la marmelade d'oranges
married marié
mascara le mascara
mass (church) la messe
mast le mât
match (light) l'allumette (f); (sport) le match
material (cloth) le tissu
matter: it doesn't matter ça ne fait rien
mattress le matelas
May mai
maybe peut-être
me: it's me c'est moi; *it's for me* c'est pour moi; *give it to me* donnez-le-moi
meal le repas
mean: what does this mean? qu'est-ce que cela veut dire?
meat la viande
mechanic le mécanicien, le garagiste
medication les médicaments (m)
medicine le médicament; (subject) le médicine
Mediterranean la Méditerranée
meeting la réunion
melon le melon
menu la carte; *set menu* le menu
message le message
microwave le micro-ondes
middle le milieu
midnight minuit
milk le lait
mine: it's mine c'est à moi
mineral water l'eau minérale (f)
minute la minute
mirror le miroir; (car) le rétroviseur
Miss Mademoiselle
mistake l'erreur (f)
mobile phone le téléphone portable
modem le modem
Monday lundi
money l'argent (m)
monitor (computer) le moniteur
month le mois
monument le monument
moon la lune
moped la mobylette
more plus; *more or less* plus ou moins
morning le matin; *in the morning* dans la matinée
mosquito le moustique
mother la mère

motorboat le bateau à moteur

motorcycle la moto

motorway l'autoroute (f)

mountain la montagne

mountain bike le vélo tout terrain

mouse la souris

mousse (hair) la mousse

moustache la moustache

mouth la bouche

move bouger; (house) déménager; *don't move!* ne bougez pas!

Mr Monsieur

Mrs Madame

mug la tasse

museum le musée

mushroom le champignon

music la musique

musical instrument l'instrument de musique (m)

musician le musicien

mussels les moules (f)

must: I must je dois

mustard la moutarde

my: my book mon livre; *my house* ma maison; *my shoes* mes chaussures

N

nail (metal) le clou; (finger) l'ongle (m)

nail clippers la pince à ongles

nailfile la lime à ongles

nail polish le vernis à ongles

name le nom; *what's your name* comment vous appelez-vous?

nappy la couche

narrow étroit

near: near the door près de la porte

necessary nécessaire

neck le cou

necklace le collier

need (verb) avoir besoin de; *I need ...* j'ai besoin de ...; *there's no need* ce n'est pas nécessaire

needle l'aiguille (f)

negative (photo) le négatif

neither: neither of them ni l'un ni l'autre; *neither ... nor ...* ni ... ni ...

nephew le neveu

never jamais

new nouveau, (fem) nouvelle; neuf, (fem) neuve

news les nouvelles (f); (television) les informations (f)

newsagent's le tabac; le tabac-journaux

newspaper le journal

next prochain; *next week* la semaine prochaine; *what next?* et puis quoi?

nice (place etc) joli; (person) sympathique

niece la nièce

night la nuit

nightclub la boîte de nuit

nightdress la chemise de nuit

nine neuf

nineteen dix-neuf

ninety quatre-vingt-dix

no (response) non; (not any) aucun

nobody personne

noisy bruyant

none aucun

noon midday

north le nord

nose le nez

not pas; *he's not ...* il n'est pas ...

notebook le carnet

notepad le bloc notes

nothing rien

novel le roman

November novembre

now maintenant

nowhere nulle part

nudist le nudiste

number (figure) le numéro; (amount) le nombre

number plate la plaque d'immatriculation

nurse infirmier; (fem) infirmière

nut (fruit) la noix; (for bolt) l'écrou (m)

O

oars les rames (f)

occasionally de temps en temps

October octobre

of de

of course bien sûr

office le bureau

often souvent

oil l'huile (f)

ointment la pommade

OK d'accord

old vieux, (fem) vieille; *how old are you?* quel âge avez-vous?

olive l'olive (f)

omelette l'omelette (f)

on ... sur ...

one un/une

onion l'oignon (m)

only seulement

open ouvert (adj); (verb) ouvrir

opening times les heures d'ouverture (f)

operating theatre la salle d'opérations

operation l'opération (f)

operator (phone) l'opérateur (m)

opposite en face de

optician's l'opticien (m)

or ou

orange (fruit) l'orange (f); (colour) orange

orange juice le jus d'orange

orchestra l'orchestre (m)

ordinary habituel

organ (music) l'orgue (m)

other: the other ... l'autre ...

our: our house notre maison; *our children* nos enfants; *it's ours* c'est à nous

out: he's out il n'est pas là

outside dehors

oven le four

over (above) au-dessus de; (more than) plus de; (finished) fini; *it's over the road* c'est de l'autre côté de la rue; *over there* là-bas

overtake (in a car) doubler

oyster l'huître (f)

P

pack of cards le jeu de cartes

package le paquet; (parcel) le colis

packet le paquet

padlock le cadenas

page la page

pain la douleur

paint la peinture

painting la peinture

pair la paire

palace le palais

pale pâle, blême

pancake la crêpe

paper le papier; (newspaper) le journal

paraffin le pétrole

parcel le colis

pardon? pardon?

parents les parents (m)

park le jardin public; (verb) garer

parting (in hair) la raie

party (celebration) la fête, la soirée;

(group) le groupe;
(political) le parti
passenger le passager
passport le passeport
passport control le
contrôle des passeports
password le mot de
passe
pasta les pâtes (f)
path le chemin,
l'allée (f)
pavement le trottoir
pay payer
payment le paiement
peach la pêche
peanuts
les cacahuètes (f)
pear la poire
pearl la perle
peas les petits pois (m)
pedestrian le piéton
peg la pince à linge
pen le stylo
pencil le crayon
pencil sharpener le
taille-crayon
penknife le canif
pen pal le
correspondant
people les gens (m)
pepper (and salt) le
poivre; (red/green) le
poivron
peppermints les
bonbons à la
menthe (m)
per: per night par nuit
perfect parfait
perfume le parfum
perhaps peut-être
perm la permanente
pet passport le
passeport d'animaux
petrol l'essence (f)
petrol station la station-
service
pets les animaux
(familiers) (m)
phonecard la carte
téléphonique
photocopier le copieur
photograph la photo;
(verb) photographier
photographer le/la
photographe
phrase book le guide
de conversation
piano le piano
pickpocket le
pickpocket
picnic le pique-nique
piece le morceau
pill le comprimé
pillow l'oreiller (m)
pilot le pilote
PIN le code
pin l'épingle (f)
pineapple l'ananas (m)
pink rose
pipe (for smoking) la
pipe; (for water) le

tuyau
piston le piston
pitch l'emplacement (m)
pizza la pizza
place l'endroit (m); *at
your place* chez vous
plant la plante
plaster le pansement
plastic le plastique
plastic bag le sac
plastic wrap le film
alimentaire
transparent
plate l'assiette (f)
platform le quai
play (theatre) la pièce;
(verb) jouer
please s'il vous plaît
*pleased: pleased to meet
you* enchanté(e)
plug (electrical) la
prise; (sink) le
bouchon
plumber (occupation)
le plombier
pocket la poche
poison le poison
police la police
police officer le policier
police report le rapport
de police
police station le
commissariat
politics la politique
poor pauvre; (bad
quality) mauvais
pop music la musique
pop
pork le porc
port (harbour) le port;
(drink) le porto
porter le porteur
possible possible
post la poste; (verb)
poster
postbox la boîte à
lettres
postcard la carte postale
postcode le code postal
poster (outside)
l'affiche (f); (inside)
le poster
postman le facteur
post office la poste
potato la pomme de
terre
poultry la volaille
pound (money,
weight) la livre
powder la poudre
pram le landau
prefer préférer
prescription
l'ordonnance (f)
pretty (beautiful) joli;
(quite) plutôt
price le prix
priest le prêtre
printer l'imprimante (f)
private privé
problem le problème

profession la profession
professor le professeur
profits
les bénéfices (m)
public le public
pull tirer
puncture la crevaison
purple violet
purse le porte-monnaie
push pousser
pushchair la poussette
put mettre
pyjamas le pyjama

Q

quality la qualité
quarter le quart
question la question
queue la queue;
(verb) faire la queue
quick rapide
quiet (preson)
silencieux; (street,
etc) tranquille
quite (fairly) assez;
(fully) très

R

rabbit le lapin
radiator le radiateur
radio la radio
radish le radis
rail: by rail par chemin
de fer
railway le chemin de
fer
rain la pluie
raincoat
l'imperméable (m)
raisin le raisin sec
rake le râteau
rare (uncommon)
rare; (steak) saignant
rash la rougeur
raspberry la framboise
rat le rat
razor blades les lames
de rasoir (f)
read lire
reading lamp la lampe
de bureau; (bedside)
la lampe de chevet
ready prêt
ready meals les plats
préparés (m)
receipt le reçu
reception la réception
receptionist le/la
receptionniste
record (music) le
disque; (sports etc)
le record
record player le tourne-
disque
record shop
le disquaire
red rouge; (hair) roux
refreshments les
rafraîchissements (m)

registered post en recommandé
relax se détendre
religion la religion
remember: I remember je m'en souviens; *I don't remember* je ne me souviens pas
rent (verb) louer
reservation la réservation
reserve (verb) réserver
rest (remainder) le reste; (verb: relax) se reposer
restaurant le restaurant
restaurant car le wagon-restaurant
return (come back) revenir; (give back) rendre
return ticket l'aller retour (m)
rice le riz
rich riche
right (correct) juste; (not left) la droite
ring (jewellery) la bague
ripe mûr
river la rivière; (big) le fleuve
road la route; (in town) la rue
roasted rôti
rock (stone) le rocher; (music) le rock
roll (bread) le petit pain
roof le toit
room la chambre; (space) la place
room service le room service
rope la corde
rose la rose
round (circular) rond; *it's my round* c'est ma tournée
roundabout le rond-point
row (verb) ramer
rowing boat la barque
rubber (material) le caoutchouc
rubbish les ordures (f); les détritus (m)
rubbish bin la poubelle
rug (mat) la carpette; (blanket) la couverture
rugby le rugby
ruins les ruines (f)
ruler la règle
rum le rhum
run (verb) courir
runway la piste

S

sad triste

safe (not in danger) en sécurité; (not dangerous) sans danger
safety pin l'épingle de nourrice (f)
sailing la voile
sailing boat le voilier
salad la salade
sale la vente; (at reduced prices) les soldes (f)
salmon le saumon
salt le sel
same: the same ... le/la même ...; *the same again, please* la même chose, s'il vous plaît
sand le sable
sandals les sandales (f)
sand dunes les dunes (f)
sandwich le sandwich
sanitary towels les serviettes hygiéniques (f)
Saturday samedi
sauce la sauce
saucer la soucoupe
saucepan la casserole
sauna le sauna
sausage la saucisse
say dire; *what did you say?* qu'avez-vous dit?; *how do you say ...?* comment dit-on ...?
scarf l'écharpe (f); (head) le foulard
schedule l'emploi du temps (m)
school l'école (f)
science la science
scissors les ciseaux (m)
Scotland l'Ecosse (f)
screen l'écran (m)
screw la vis
screwdriver le tournevis
sea la mer
seafood les fruits de mer (m)
seat la place
seat belt la ceinture de sécurité
second (of time) la seconde; (in series) deuxième
second class en seconde
secretary le/la secrétaire
see voir; *I can't see* je ne vois rien; *I see* je vois
self-employed à mon compte
sell vendre
seminar le séminaire
send envoyer
separate séparé (adj); (verb) séparer
September septembre
serious sérieux
seven sept
seventeen dix-sept

seventy soixante-dix
several plusieurs
sew coudre
shampoo le shampooing
shave: to shave se raser
shaving foam la mousse à raser
shawl le châle
she elle
sheet le drap
shell la coquille
shellfish les crustacés (m)
ship le bateau
shirt la chemise
shoelaces les lacets (m)
shoemaker la cordonnerie
shoe polish le cirage
shoes les chaussures (f)
shop le magasin
shopkeeper commerçant; (fem) commerçante
shopping les courses (f); *to go shopping* faire les courses
short court; petit
shorts le short
shoulder l'épaule (f)
shower (bath) la douche; (rain) l'averse (f)
shower gel le gel douche
shrimp la crevette
shutter (camera) l'obturateur (m); (window) le volet
sick: I feel sick j'ai envie de vomir; *to be sick* (vomit) vomir
side (edge) le bord
sidelights les feux de position (m)
sightseeing le tourism
silk la soie
silver (colour) argenté; (metal) l'argent (m)
simple simple
sing chanter
single (one) seul; (unmarried) célibataire
single room la chambre pour une personne; la chambre simple
single ticket l'aller simple (m)
sink l'évier (m)
sir monsieur
sister la sœur
six six
sixteen seize
sixty soixante
size la taille
skates les patins à glace (m)
ski le ski; (verb) skier
ski boots les chaussures de ski (f)

skid (verb) déraper

skiing: to go skiing faire du ski

ski lift le remonte-pente

skin cleanser le démaquillant

ski pole le bâton de ski

ski resort la station de ski

skirt la jupe

sky le ciel

sled la luge

sleep le sommeil; (verb) dormir

sleeper le wagon-lit

sleeping bag le sac de couchage

sleeping pill le somnifère

sleeve la manche

slip le jupon

slippers les pantoufles (f)

slow lent

small petit

smell l'odeur (f); (verb) sentir

smile le sourire; (verb) sourire

smoke la fumée; (verb) fumer

snack le snack

snow la neige

so si

soaking solution (for contact lenses) la solution de trempage

soap le savon

socks les chaussettes (f)

soft mou

soft lenses les lentilles souples (f)

soil la terre

somebody quelqu'un

somehow d'une façon ou d'une autre

something quelque chose

sometimes quelquefois

somewhere quelque part

son le fils

song la chanson

sorry (apology) pardon; *sorry?* (pardon?) pardon?; *I'm sorry* je suis désolé

soup la soupe

south le sud

souvenir le souvenir

spade (shovel) la pelle; (garden) la bêche

spades (cards) pique

Spain l'Espagne (f)

Spanish espagnol

spare parts les pièces de rechange (f)

spark plug la bougie

speak parler; *do you speak …?* parlez-vous …?; *I don't speak …* je ne parle pas …

speed la vitesse

speed limit la limitation de vitesse

spider l'araignée (f)

spinach les épinards (m)

spoon la cuillère

sport le sport

sports centre le centre sportif

spring (mechanical) le ressort; (season) le printemps

square (in town) la place; (adj: shape) carré

stadium le stade

staircase l'escalier (m)

stairs les escaliers (m)

stamp le timbre

stapler l'agrafeuse (f)

star l'étoile (f); (movie) la vedette

start (beginning) le début; (verb) commencer

starters les entrées (f)

statement la déposition

station la gare; (underground) la station

statue la statue

steak le steak

steal voler; *it's been stolen* on l'a volé

steamed à la vapeur

steamer le bateau à vapeur; (cooking) le couscoussier

steering wheel le volant

sting la piqûre; (verb) piquer

stockings les bas (m)

stomach l'estomac (m)

stomach ache le mal de ventre, le mal à l'estomac

stop (bus) l'arrêt (de bus) (m); (verb) s'arrêter

storm la tempête

straight on tout droit

strawberry la fraise

stream (small river) le ruisseau

street la rue

street musician le musicien des rues

string (cord) la ficelle; (guitar etc) la corde

strong (person, drink) fort; (material) résistant

student l'étudiant (m)

stupid stupide

suburbs la banlieue

sugar le sucre

suit le costume; *it suits you* ça vous va bien

suitcase la valise

summer l'été (m)

sun le soleil

sunbathe se faire bronzer

sunburn le coup de soleil

Sunday dimanche

sunglasses les lunettes de soleil (f)

sunny ensoleillé

sunshade le parasol

suntan le bronzage

suntan lotion la lotion solaire

supermarket le supermarché

supper le souper

supplement le supplément

suppository le suppositoire

sure sûr

surname le nom de famille

sweat la transpiration; (verb) transpirer

sweater le pull

sweatshirt le sweat-shirt

sweet (not sour) sucré; (confectionery) le bonbon

swim (verb) nager

swimming la natation; *to go swimming* aller se baigner

swimming pool la piscine

swimming trunks le maillot de bain

swimsuit le maillot de bain

Swiss suisse(sse)

switch l'interrupteur (m)

Switzerland la Suisse

synagogue la synagogue

syringe la seringue

syrup le sirop

T

table la table

tablet le cachet

take prendre

take away: to take away à emporter

takeoff le décollage

talcum powder le talc

talk la conversation; (verb) parler

tall grand

tampon le tampon

tangerine la mandarine

tap (water) le robinet

tapestry la tapisserie

taxi le taxi

tea le thé

teacher (secondary)

le professeur
telephone le téléphone; (verb) téléphoner
telephone box la cabine téléphonique
television la télévision
temperature la température
ten dix
tennis le tennis
tent la tente
tent peg le piquet de tente
tent pole le montant de tente
terminal le terminal
terrace la terrasse
than que
thank (verb) remercier; *thank you* merci; *thanks* merci
that (that one) ça; *that bus* ce bus; *that man* cet homme; *that woman* cette femme; *what's that?* qu'est-ce que c'est?; *I think that the* ... je pense que le ...
the le/la; (plural) les
theatre le théâtre
their: their room leur chambre; *their books* leurs livres; *it's theirs* c'est à eux
them: it's them ce sont eux/elles; *it's for them* c'est pour eux/elles; *give it to them* donnez-le-leur
then alors; (after) ensuite
there là; *there is/are* ... il y a ...
these: these things ces choses; *these are mine* ils sont à moi
they ils; (fem) elles
thick épais
thief le voleur
thin mince, maigre
think penser; *I think so* je pense que oui; *I'll think about it* je vais y penser
third troisième
thirsty: I'm thirsty j'ai soif
thirteen treize
thirty trente
this (this one) ceci; *this bus* ce bus; *this man* cet homme; *this woman* cette femme; *what's this?* qu'est-ce que c'est?; *this is Mr* ... je vous présente M. ...
those: those things ces choses-là; *those are his* ils sont à lui

three trois
throat la gorge
throat pastilles les pastilles pour la gorge (f)
through à travers
thunderstorm l'orage (m)
Thursday jeudi
ticket le billet; (underground, bus) le ticket
ticket collector le contrôleur
ticket office le guichet
tide la marée
tie la cravate; (verb) nouer
tight étroit
tights les collants (m)
tiles, tiling le carrelage
time l'heure (f); *what's the time?* quelle heure est-il?
timetable (train, bus) l'horaire (f)
tip (money) le pourboire; (end) le bout
tired fatigué
tissues mouchoirs
to: to England en Angleterre; *to Paris* à Paris; *to the station* à la gare; *to the centre* au centre; *to the doctor* chez le docteur
toast le pain grillé
tobacco le tabac
toboggan le toboggan
today aujourd'hui
together ensemble
toilet paper le papier hygiénique
toilets les toilettes (f)
tomato la tomate
tomorrow demain; *see you tomorrow* à demain
tongue la langue
tonic le tonic
tonight ce soir
too (also) aussi; (excessively) trop
tooth la dent
toothache le mal de dents
toothbrush la brosse à dents
toothpaste le dentifrice
torch la lampe de poche
tour la visite
tourist le/la touriste
tourist office le syndicat d'initiative
towel la serviette
tower la tour
town la ville
town centre le centre-ville
town hall l'hôtel de ville

(m); la mairie
toy le jouet
track suit le survêtement
tractor le tracteur
trade fair la foire-exposition
tradition la tradition
traffic la circulation, le trafic
traffic lights les feux (m)
trailer la remorque
train le train
trainee le stagiaire
trainers les tennis (m)
translate traduire
translator le traducteur
travel agency l'agence de voyages (f)
traveller's cheque le chèque de voyage
tray le plateau
tree l'arbre (m)
trolley le chariot
trousers le pantalon
truck le camion
true vrai
try essayer
Tuesday mardi
tunnel le tunnel
tweezers la pince à épiler
twelve douze
twenty vingt
two deux
tyre le pneu

U

ugly laid
umbrella le parapluie
uncle l'oncle (m)
under ... sous ...
underground le métro
underpants le slip
understand comprendre; *I understand* je comprends; *I don't understand* je ne comprends pas
underwear les sous-vêtements (m)
university l'université (f)
university lecturer le maître de conférences
unleaded sans plomb
until jusqu'à
unusual inhabituel
up en haut; (upward) vers le haut; *up there* là-haut
urgent urgent
us: it's us c'est nous; *it's for us* c'est pour nous; *give it to us* donnez-le-nous
use (verb) utiliser; *it's no use* ça ne sert à rien
useful utile

usual habituel
usually d'habitude

V

vacancy (room) la chambre à louer
vaccination la vaccination
vacuum cleaner l'aspirateur (m)
valley la vallée
valve la soupape
vanilla la vanille
vase le vase
VCR le magnétoscope
veal le veau
vegetables les légumes (m)
vegetarian (adj) végétarien
vehicle le véhicule
very très; *very much* beaucoup
vet le vétérinaire
video (film/tape) la vidéo
view la vue
viewfinder le viseur
villa la villa
village le village
vinegar le vinaigre
violin le violon
visit la visite; (verb: place) visiter; (person) rendre visite
visitor le visiteur
vitamin pill le comprimé de vitamines
vodka la vodka
voice la voix
voicemail la messagerie téléphonique

W

wait attendre; *wait!* attendez!
waiter le serveur; *waiter!* garçon!
waiting room la salle d'attente
waitress la serveuse; *waitress!* Mademoiselle!
Wales le pays de Galles
walk (verb) marcher; *to go for a walk* aller se promener
wall (inside) la paroi; (outside) le mur
wallet le portefeuille
want (verb) vouloir; *I would like* je voudrais
war la guerre
wardrobe l'armoire (f)
warm chaud
was: I was j'étais; *he was* il était; *she was* elle était; *it was* il/elle était
washer la rondelle

washing machine la machine à laver
washing powder la lessive
washing-up liquid le produit pour la vaisselle
wasp la guêpe
watch la montre; (verb) regarder
water l'eau (f)
waterfall la chute d'eau
water heater le chauffe-eau
wave la vague; (verb) faire signe de la main
wavy (hair) ondulé
we nous
weather le temps
Web site le site web
wedding le mariage
Wednesday mercredi
weeds les mauvais herbes (f)
week la semaine
welcome: you're welcome je vous en prie
Wellington boots les boîtes en caoutchouc (f)
were: we were nous étions; *you were* vous étiez; *they were* ils/elles étaient
west l'ouest
wet mouillé
what? comment?; *what is it?* qu'est-ce que c'est?
wheel la roue
wheelchair le fauteuil roulant; la chaise roulante
when? quand?
where? où?
whether si
which? lequel?
whisky le whisky
white blanc, (fem) blanche
who? qui?
why? pourquoi?
wide large
wife la femme
wind le vent
window la fenêtre
windscreen le pare-brise
wine le vin
wine list la carte des vins
wine merchant le négociant en vins
wing l'aile (f)
winter l'hiver (m)
with avec; *with pleasure* avec plasir
withdraw (verb) retirer
without sans
witness le témoin

woman la femme
wood le bois
wool la laine
word le mot
work le travail; (verb) travailler; (machine etc) fonctionner
worktop le plan de travail
worse pire
worst le pire
wrapping paper le papier d'emballage; (for presents) le papier cadeau
wrench la clé anglaise
wrist le poignet
write (verb) écrire; *written by* écrit par
writing paper le papier à lettres
wrong faux, (fem) fausse

X, Y, Z

x-ray radio
x-ray departement la salle de radiology
year l'an (m); l'année (f)
yellow jaune
yes oui
yesterday hier
yet déjà; *not yet* pas encore
yoghurt le yaourt
you (singular informal) tu; (plural; singular formal) vous
young jeune
your (singular informal): *your book* ton livre; *your house* ta maison; *your shoes* tes chaussures; *it's yours* c'est à toi; (plural; singular formal): *your house* votre maison; *your shoes* vos chaussures; *it's yours* c'est à vous
youth hostel l'auberge de jeunesse (f)
zip la fermeture éclair
zoo le zoo

Dictionary
French *to English*

The gender of French nouns listed here is indicated by the abbreviations "(m)" and "(f)", for masculine and feminine. Plural nouns are indicated by "(m pl)" or "(f pl)". French adjectives (adj) vary according to the gender and number of the word they describe; the masculine form is shown here. In most cases, you add an **-e** to the masculine form to make it feminine. Certain endings use a different rule: masculine adjectives that end in **-x** adopt an **-se** ending in the feminine form, while those that end in **-ien** change to **-ienne**. Some feminine adjectives that do not follow these rules are shown here and follow the abbreviation "(fem)". For the plural form, a (silent) **-s** is usually added.

A

à: *at:* à la poste *at the post office;* à trois heures *at 3 o'clock;* à côté de *beside;* à demain *see you tomorrow;* à emporter *to take away;* à travers *through*

abat-jour (m) *lampshade*

abricot (m) *apricot*

accélérateur (m) *accelerator*

accident (m) *accident*

acheter *to buy*

adaptateur (m) *adaptor* (voltage)

addition (f) *bill*

adhésif (m) *adhesive*

adresse (f) *address*

adresse électronique (f) *email address*

aéroglisseur (m) *hovercraft*

aéroport (m) *airport*

affaire (f) *bargain*

affaires (f pl) *business*

affiche (f) *poster* (outside)

affreux *awful*

agence de voyages (f) *travel agency*

agenda (m) *diary*

agent (m) *agent*

agneau (m) *lamb*

agrafeuse (f) *stapler*

agrandissement (m) *enlargement*

aide (f) *help*

aider *to help*

aiguille (f) *needle;* aiguille à tricoter *knitting needle*

ail (m) *garlic*

aile (f) *wing*

ailleurs *somewhere else*

aimer *to like/love;* j'aime nager *I like swimming;* je n'aime pas *I don't like*

air (m) *air*

alcool (m) *alcohol*

Algérie (f) *Algeria*

algérien(ne) *Algerian*

allée (f) *path*

Allemagne (f) *Germany*

allemand(e) *German*

aller *to go*

aller chercher *to get* (fetch)

allergique *allergic*

aller patiner *to go ice-skating*

aller retour (m) *return ticket*

aller simple (m) *single ticket*

allez-vous en! *go away!*

allumage (m) *ignition*

allumette (f) *match* (light)

alors *well then*

Alpes: les Alpes (m pl) *Alps*

amant (m) *lover*

ambassade (f) *embassy*

ambulance (f) *ambulance*

amer *bitter*

américain(e) *American*

Amérique (f) *America*

ami(e) *friend*

amical *friendly*

amour (m) *love*

amphithéâtre (m) *lecture theatre*

ampoule (f) *blister; light bulb*

an (m) *year*

ananas (m) *pineapple*

Andorre *Andorra*

anglais(e) *English*

Angleterre (f) *England*

animaux (familiers) (m pl) *pets*

animé *busy* (street)

année (f) *year*

anniversaire (m) *birthday*

annuaire (m) *directory* (telephone)

antigel (m) *antifreeze*

antiseptique (m) *antiseptic*

août *August*

apéritif (m) *aperitif*

appareil acoustique (m) *hearing aid*

appareil-photo (m) *camera*

appartement (m) *apartment*

appât (m) *bait*

appétit (m) *appetite*

apprendre *to learn*

après *after*

après-midi (m) *afternoon*

après-rasage (m) *aftershave*

araignée (f) *spider*

arbre (m) *tree*

arbre à cames (m) *camshaft*

architecture (f) *architecture*

arête (f) *fishbone*

argent (m) *cash; money; silver* (metal)

argenté *silver* (colour)

armoire (f) *wardrobe*

arrêt de bus (m) *bus stop*

arrière (m) *back (not front)*
arrivée (f) *arrival*
arriver *to arrive*
art (m) *art*
artiste (m) *artist*
ascenseur (m) *lift*
aspirateur (m) *vacuum cleaner*
aspirine (f) *aspirin*
assez *enough; fairly*
assiette (f) *plate*
assurance (f) *insurance*
asthmatique *asthmatic*
attaché-case (m) *briefcase*
attendez! *wait!*
attendre *to wait*
attention! *careful!*
atterrir *to land*
attirant *attractive*
au: au café *at the café*; au revoir *goodbye*
auberge (f) *inn*
auberge de jeunesse (f) *youth hostel*
aucun *not any; none*
au-dessus de *over (above)*
aujourd'hui *today*
aussi *too (also)*
Australie (f) *Australia*
australien(ne) *Australian*
automatique *automatic*
automne (m) *autumn*
autoroute (f) *motorway*
autre: autre chose *something else*
avance (f) *advance*
avant *before*
avec *with;* avec plaisir *with pleasure*
averse (f) *shower (rain)*
aveugle *blind (cannot see)*
avion (m) *aircraft*
avocat (m) *avocado*
avocat(e) *lawyer*
avoir *to have*
avril *April*

B

bac (m) *ferry (small)*
bagages (m pl) *luggage; baggage;* bagages à main (m pl) *hand luggage*
baigner: aller se baigner *to go swimming*
bain (m) *bath*
balai (m) *broom*
balcon (m) *balcony*

balle (f) *ball (tennis etc)*
ballon (m) *ball (football etc)*
banane (f) *banana*
bandage (m) *bandage*
banlieue (f) *suburbs*
banque (f) *bank*
bar (m) *bar (place)*
barbe (f) *beard*
barbecue (m) *barbecue*
barque (f) *rowing boat*
bas (m) *stockings; low (adj);* en bas *down*
bateau (m) *boat; ship;* bateau à moteur (m) *motorboat;* bateau à vapeur (m) *steamer*
bâtiment (m) *building*
bâton de ski (m) *ski pole*
batterie (f) *battery (car)*
baume après-shampooing (m) *conditioner (hair)*
beau, (fem) belle *beautiful*
bébé (m) *baby*
bêche (f) *spade (garden)*
beige *beige*
beignet (m) *doughnut*
belge *Belgian*
Belgique: la Belgique *Belgium*
bénéfices (m pl) *profits*
béquilles (f pl) *crutches*
besoin: avoir besoin de *to need;* j'ai besoin de ... *I need ...*
beurre (m) *butter*
bibliothèque (f) *library*
bicyclette (f) *bicycle*
bien sûr *of course*
bien! *good!;* ça vous va bien *it suits you*
bière (f) *beer*
bijouterie (f) *jeweller's*
billet (m) *ticket; banknote*
biscuit (m) *biscuit*
blanc, (fem) blanche *white*
blanchisserie (f) *laundry (place)*
blême *pale*
blessure (f) *injury*
bleu (m) *bruise;* blue (adj)
bloc notes (m) *notepad*
blond (adj) *blond*
bœuf (m) *beef*
boire *to drink;* vous voulez boire quelque chose? *would you like something to drink?*
bois (m) *wood*
boisson (f) *drink*
boîte (f) *box;* boîte à lettres *postbox;* boîte

de chocolats *box of chocolates;* boîte de conserve *can (vessel);* boîte de nuit *nightclub;* boîte de vitesses *gearbox*
boîtes en caoutchouc (f pl) *Wellington boots*
bol (m) *bowl*
bon, (fem) bonne *good*
bonbon (m) *sweet (confectionery);* bonbons à la menthe (m pl) *peppermints*
bondé *crowded*
bonjour *hello*
bon marché *inexpensive; cheap*
bonne chance! *good luck!*
bonsoir *good evening*
bord (m) *side (edge)*
botte (f) *boot (footwear)*
bouche (f) *mouth*
boucherie (f) *butcher's*
bouchon (m) *plug (sink); cork*
boucles (f pl) *curls*
boucles d'oreille (f pl) *earrings*
bouger *to move;* ne bougez pas! *don't move!*
bougie (f) *spark plug; candle*
bouilli *boiled*
bouillir *to boil*
bouilloire (f) *kettle*
boulangerie (f) *bakery*
bout (m) *tip, end*
bouteille (f) *bottle*
bouton (m) *button;* boutons de manchette (m pl) *cuff links*
bracelet (m) *bracelet*
branche (f) *branch*
bras (m) *arm*
Bretagne: la Bretagne *Brittany*
bretelles (f pl) *braces (clothes)*
briquet (m) *lighter*
britannique *British*
broche (f) *brooch*
brochure (f) *brochure*
broderie (f) *embroidery*
bronzage (m) *suntan*
bronzer: se faire bronzer *to sunbathe*
brosse (f) *brush;* brosse à dents (f) *toothbrush*
brosser *to brush*
brouillard (m) *fog*
brûler *to burn*
brûlure (f) *burn*
Bruxelles *Brussels*
bruyant *noisy*
budget (m) *budget*
bunker (m) *bunker*

C

bureau (m) *desk; office*
bureau de location (m) *box office*
bus (m) *bus*

ça *that (that one)*
cabine téléphonique (f) *telephone box*
cacahuètes (f pl) *peanuts*
cachet (m) *tablet*
cadeau (m) *gift*
cadenas (m) *padlock*
cadre (m) *executive (in company)*
cafard (m) *cockroach*
café (m) *café; coffee*; café crème *white coffee*; café soluble *instant coffee*
cage (f) *cage*
caisse (f) *check-out (supermarket)*
calculette (f) *calculator*
cambriolage (m) *burglary*
caméscope (m) *camcorder*
camion (m) *truck*
campagne (f) *countryside*
camping-car (m) *camper van*
Canada (m) *Canada*
canadien(ne) *Canadian*
canal (m) *canal*
canif (m) *penknife*
canne à pêche (f) *fishing rod*
canoë (m) *canoe*
caoutchouc (m) *rubber (material)*
capot (m) *car bonnet*
capsule (f) *cap (bottle)*
caravane (f) *caravan*
carburateur (m) *carburettor*
carnet (m) *notebook*; carnet de chèques (m) *chequebook*
carotte (f) *carrot*
carpette (f) *rug (mat)*
carré *square (adj: shape)*
carreau *diamonds (cards)*
carrelage (m) *tiles, tiling*
carte (f) *menu; card; map;* carte bancaire *debit card;* carte de crédit *credit card;* carte d'embarquement *boarding pass;*carte des vins *wine list;* carte de visite *business card;* carte postale

postcard; carte téléphonique *phonecard*
casquette (f) *cap (hat)*
cassé *broken*
casserole (f) *saucepan*
cassette (f) *cassette*
cassis (m) *blackcurrant*
cathédrale (f) *cathedral*
cave (f) *cellar*
ce (bus) *that (bus)*
ceci *this (this one)*
ceinture (f) *belt;* ceinture de sécurité *seat belt*
célibataire *single (unmarried)*
cellule photoélectrique (f) *light meter*
cendrier (m) *ashtray*
cent *hundred*
centre (m) *centre;* centre sportif (m) *sports centre*
centre-ville (m) *town centre*
cerise (f) *cherry*
certificat (m) *certificate*
ces (choses) *these (things)*
c'est *it's;* c'est tout *that's all*
cet (homme) *that (man)*
cette (femme) *that (woman)*
chaise (f) *chair*
châle (m) *shawl*
chambre (f) *bedroom;* chambre à louer *vacancy;* chambre pour deux personnes *double room;* chambre simple *single room*
chambre à air (f) *inner tube*
champ (m) *field (farming)*
champignon (m) *mushroom*
chance (f) *luck*
changer *to change (money);* se changer *to change (clothes)*
chanson (f) *song*
chanter *to sing*
chapeau (m) *hat*
chaque *each; every*
charcuterie (f) *delicatessen*
chargeur (m) *charger*
chariot (m) *trolley*
charpentier (m) *carpenter*
chat (m) *cat*
château (m) *castle*
chaud *hot; warm;* j'ai chaud *I feel hot*

chauffage (m) *heating;* chauffage central *central heating*
chauffe-eau (m) *boiler; water heater*
chaussettes (f pl) *socks*
chaussures (f pl) *shoes;* chaussures de ski (f pl) *ski boots*
chauve *bald*
chef (m) *manager;* chef d'orchestre *conductor (orchestra);* chef de train *guard (train)*
chemin (m) *path*
chemin de fer (m) *railway*
cheminée (f) *fireplace; chimney*
chemise (f) *shirt;* chemise de nuit *nightdress*
chemisier (m) *blouse*
chèque (m) *cheque;* chèque de voyage *traveller's cheque*
cher *expensive;* pas cher *inexpensive*
cheveux (m pl) *hair;* les cheveux longs/courts *long/short hair*
cheville (f) *ankle*
chez *at home;* chez moi *at my house;* chez vous *at your place*
chien (m) *dog*
chiffon à poussière (m) *duster*
chiffres (m pl) *figures*
chips (f pl) *crisps*
chocolat (m) *chocolate*
chou (m) *cabbage*
chou-fleur (m) *cauliflower*
chute d'eau (f) *waterfall*
ciel (m) *sky*
cigare (m) *cigar*
cigarette (f) *cigarette*
cimetière (m) *cemetery*
cinéma (m) *cinema*
cinq *five*
cinquante *fifty*
cintre (m) *coat hanger*
cirage (m) *shoe polish*
circulation (f) *traffic*
ciseaux (m pl) *scissors*
citron (m) *lemon;* citron vert *lime*
clair *clear; light (not dark)*
classe (f) *class*
clavier (m) *keyboard*
clé (f) *key;* clé anglaise (f) *wrench*
clignotant (m) *indicator*

climatisation (f) *air conditioning*

cloche (f) *bell* (church)

clou (m) *nail* (metal)

cocktail (m) *cocktail party*

code (m) *PIN*

code de la route (m) *highway code*

code postal (m) *postcode*

cœur (m) *heart;* problème au cœur *heart condition;* cœurs (m pl) *hearts* (cards)

coffre (m) *boot* (car)

cognac (m) *brandy*

coiffeur (m) *hairdresser; barber's*

coin (m) *corner*

col (m) *collar*

colis (m) *parcel*

collants (m pl) *tights*

colle (f) *glue*

collection (f) *collection* (stamps etc)

collier (m) *collar; necklace*

colline (f) *hill*

combien? *how much?;* combien ça coûte? *how much does it cost?*

comme *like* (similar to)

commencer *to start*

comment? *how?;* comment allez-vous? *how are you?;* comment est-ce que ça s'appelle? *what's it called?;* comment vous appelez-vous? *what's your name?*

commerçant(e) *shopkeeper*

commissariat (m) *police station*

commode (f) *chest of drawers*

compagnie (f) *company;* compagnie aérienne *airline*

compartiment (m) *compartment*

complet *full*

compliqué *complicated*

comprendre *to understand;* je comprends *I understand;* je ne comprends pas *I don't understand*

comprimé (m) *pill;* comprimé de vitamines *vitamin pill*

comptable (m/f) *accountant*

compte: à mon compte *self-employed*

concert (m) *concert*

concierge (m/f) *caretaker*

concombre (m) *cucumber*

conducteur (m) *driver*

conduire *to drive*

conférence (f) *conference*

confiseur (m) *confectioner*

confiture (f) *jam*

congélateur (m) *freezer*

connaître *to know* (person)

consigne automatique (f) *luggage lockers*

constructeur (m) *builder*

consulat (m) *consulate*

consultant(e) *consultant*

contraceptif (m) *contraceptive*

contre *against*

contrôle des passeports (m) *passport control*

contrôleur (m) *ticket collector*

conversation (f) *talk*

copieur (m) *photocopier*

coquille (f) *shell*

corde (f) *rope; string* (guitar etc)

cordonnerie (f) *shoemaker*

corne (f) *horn* (animal)

corps (m) *body*

correspondant (m) *pen pal*

corse *Corsican*

Corse: la Corse *Corsica*

costume (m) *suit*

côtelette (f) *chop* (food)

coton (m) *cotton;* coton hydrophile *cotton balls*

cou (m) *neck*

couche (f) *nappy;* couches à jeter (f pl) *disposable nappies*

coude (m) *elbow*

coudre *to sew*

couette (f) *duvet*

couleur (f) *colour*

couloir (m) *corridor*

coup de soleil (m) *sunburn*

coupe (de cheveux) (f) *haircut*

couper *to cut, chop*

coupure (f) *cut*

courant (m) *current*

courgette (f) *courgette*

courir *to run*

courroie du ventilateur (f) *fan belt*

courses (f pl) *shopping; to go shopping* faire les courses

court *short*

couscoussier (m) *steamer* (cooking)

cousin (m) *cousin*

couteau (m) *knife*

coûter *to cost*

couverture (f) *blanket; rug*

crabe (m) *crab*

crampe (f) *cramp*

cravate (f) *tie*

crayon (m) *pencil*

crème (f) *cream;* crème anti-insecte (f) *insect repellent cream*

crêpe (f) *pancake*

crevaison (f) *puncture*

crevette (f) *shrimp*

crier *to cry* (shout)

croisière (f) *cruise*

crustacés (m) *shellfish*

cuillère (f) *spoon*

cuir (m) *leather*

cuire *to bake*

cuisine (f) *kitchen*

cuisinier (m) *cook*

cuisinière (f) *cooker*

curry (m) *curry*

D

d'accord *OK*

danger *danger;* sans danger *safe*

dans *in*

danse (f) *dance*

danser *to dance*

de *of*

début (m) *start* (beginning)

débutant(e) *beginner*

décapsuleur (m) *bottle opener*

décembre *December*

décollage (m) *takeoff*

décolorer *to bleach*

décorateur (m) *decorator*

dehors *outside*

déjà *yet; already*

déjeuner (m) *lunch*

delco (m) *distributor* (car)

demain *tomorrow*

démaquillant (m) *skin cleanser*

déménager *to move house*

demi *half;* une demi-heure *half an hour*

demi-pension (f) *half board*

dent (f) *tooth*
dentelle (f) *lace*
dentier (m) *dentures*
dentifrice (m)
  toothpaste
dentiste (m/f) *dentist*
déodorant (m)
  deodorant
départ (m) *departures*
département (f)
  department
dépliant (m) *leaflet*
déposition (f)
  statement
déraper *skid* (verb)
dernier *last (final);* la
  semaine dernière *last
  week*
derrière *behind*
descendre *to get off*
  (bus etc)
designer (m) *designer*
désolé: je suis désolé(e)
  I'm sorry
desserts (m pl)
  desserts
détritus (m) *rubbish*
deux *two;* les deux *both*
deuxième *second* (in
  series)
devant *in front of*
développer *to develop*
d'habitude *usually*
diabétique *diabetic*
diamant (m) *diamond*
  (jewel)
diarrhée (f)
  diarrhoea
dictionnaire (m)
  dictionary
diesel (m) *diesel*
différent *different;*
  c'est différent *that's
  different*
difficile *difficult*
dimanche *Sunday*
dîner (m) *dinner*
dire *to say;* qu'avez-
  vous dit? *what did
  you say?;* comment
  dit-on ...? *how do
  you say ...?;* qu'est-ce
  que cela veut dire?
  what does this mean?
directeur (m)
  director
discothèque (m) *disco*
disquaire (m) *record
  shop*
disque (m) *record*
  (music); disque
  compact (m) *compact
  disc*
distributeur
  automatique (m)
  cash machine
divertissement (m)
  entertainment
divorcé *divorced*
dix *ten*
dix-huit *eighteen*

dix-neuf *nineteen*
dix-sept *seventeen*
docteur (m) *doctor*
document (m)
  document
doigt (m) *finger*
dois: je dois ... *I must ...*
dollar (m) *dollar*
donner *give*
dormir *to sleep*
dos (m) *back* (body)
douane (f) *customs*
doubler *to overtake*
  (in a car)
douche (f) *shower*
  (bath)
douleur (f) *ache; pain*
douze *twelve*
drap (m) *sheet*
drapeau (m) *flag*
draps (m pl) *bed linen*
droit (m) *law*
droite *right* (not left)
drôle *funny*
dunes (f pl) *sand
  dunes*
dur *hard*

E

eau (f) *water;* eau
  gazeuse *fizzy water;*
  eau minérale *mineral
  water;* eau potable
  drinking water; eau
  de Javel *bleach*
échanger *to exchange*
écharpe (f) *scarf*
échecs (m pl) *chess*
école (f) *school*
Ecosse: l'Ecosse (f)
  Scotland
écouteurs (m)
  headphones
écran (m) *screen*
écrevisse (f) *crayfish*
  (freshwater)
écrire *to write;* écrit
  par ... *written by ...*
écrou (m) *nut* (for
  bolt)
église (f) *church*
élastique (m) *elastic
  band;* elastic (adj)
électricien(ne)
  electrician
électricité (f) *electricity*
électrique *electric*
elle *she*
elles *they* (fem)
email (m) *email*
embrayage (m) *clutch*
émeraude (f) *emerald*
emplacement (m)
  pitch
emploi du temps (m)
  schedule
en *in;* en France *in
  France*
enchanté(e) *pleased to
  meet you*

encore: encore un café
  another coffee
encre (f) *ink*
endormi *asleep*
endroit (m) *place*
enfant (m) *child*
enfin! *at last!*
ennuyeux *boring*
enregistrement (m)
  check-in;
  enregistrement des
  bagages *baggage
  check-in*
ensemble *together*
ensoleillé *sunny*
ensuite *then (after)*
entendre *hear*
entre ... *between ...*
entrée (f) *entrance*
entrées (f pl) *starters*
enveloppe (f)
  envelope
envie: j'ai envie de ...
  I feel like ...
environ *about*
envoyer *to send*
épais *thick*
épaule (f) *shoulder*
épicerie (f) *grocer's*
épileptique *epileptic*
épinards (m) *spinach*
épingle (f) *pin;*
  épingle de nourrice
  safety pin
erreur (f) *mistake*
escalier (m) *stairs;
  staircase;* escalier
  roulant *escalator*
Espagne: l'Espagne (f)
  Spain
espagnol *Spanish*
essayer *to try*
essence (f) *petrol*
essieu (m) *axle*
est (m) *east*
est *is;* il/elle est *he/she
  is;* c'est *it is*
estimation (f)
  estimate
estomac (m) *stomach*
et *and*
étage (m) *floor*
  (storey)
été (m) *summer*
étiquette (f) *label*
étoile (f) *star*
étouffant *close* (stuffy)
étranger (m)
  foreigner
étroit *narrow; tight*
étudiant (m) *student*
eux: c'est à eux *it's
  theirs;* c'est pour
  eux/elles *it's for them*
evanouir *to faint*
évier (m) *sink*
excédent de bagages
  (m) *excess baggage*
excellent *excellent*
excursion (f)
  excursion

exemple (m) *example*

exposition (f) *exhibition*

exprès *deliberately*

extérieure (m) *exterior*; *exterior* (adj) *exterior* extincteur (m) *fire extinguisher*

F

face: en face de *opposite*

facile *easy*

façon: d'une façon ou d'une autre *somehow*

facteur (m) *postman*

facture (f) *invoice*

faim: j'ai faim *I'm hungry*

faire *to do; make*; faire de autostop *to hitchhike*; faire du jogging *to jog*; faire enregistrer ses bagages *to check in*; faire la cuisine *to cook*; faire la queue *to queue* (verb); faire signe de la main *to wave*

fan (m/f) *fan* (enthusiast)

fantastique *fantastic*

farine (f) *flour*

fatigué *tired*

fauteuil (m) *armchair*; fauteuil roulant (m) *wheelchair*

faux, (fem) fausse *wrong*

fax (m) *fax; fax machine*

félicitations! *congratulations!*

femme (f) *woman; wife*; femme de chambre *maid*; femme de ménages *cleaner*

fenêtre (f) *window*

fer à repasser (m) *iron* (for clothes)

ferme (f) *farm*

fermé *closed*

fermer *to close*

fermeture éclair (f) *zip*

fermier (m) *farmer*

ferry (m) *ferry* (large)

fête (f) *party* (celebration)

feu (m) *fire*; feu d'artifice *fireworks*; feu de camp *campfire*

feuille (f) *leaf*

feutre (m) *felt-tip pen*

feux (m pl) *lights*; *traffic lights*; feux de position (m pl) *sidelights*

fevrier *February*

fiancé *engaged* (couple)

fiancé(e) *fiancé(e)*

ficelle (f) *string* (cord)

fièvre (f) *fever*

figue (f) *fig*

fille (f) *girl; daughter*

film (m) *film*

fils (m) *son*

fin (f) *end*

fini *over* (finished)

flash (m) *flash* (camera)

fleur (f) *flower*

fleuriste (f) *florist*

fleuve (m) *river* (big)

flûte (f) *flute*

foie (m) *liver*

foire (f) *fair*; foire-exposition *trade fair*

foncé *dark*; bleu foncé *dark blue*

fonctionner *function* (machine, etc)

fond (m) *bottom*

football (m) *football*

forêt (f) *forest*

formulaire de demande (m) *application form*

fort *loud; strong* (person, drink)

fou, (fem) folle *mad*

foulard (m) *headscarf*

four (m) *oven*

fourchette (f) *fork*

frais, (fem) fraîche *cool*

fraise (f) *strawberry*

framboise (f) *raspberry*

français(e) *French*

France: la France *France*

frange (f) *fringe*

frein (m) *brake*; frein à main *handbrake*

freiner *to brake*

frère (m) *brother*

frigo (m) *fridge*

frire *to fry*

frit *fried*

frites (f pl) *chips*

froid (adj) *cold*

fromage (m) *cheese*

fromagerie (f) *cheese shop*

frontière (f) *border*

fruit (m) *fruit*

fruits de mer (m pl) *seafood*

fumée (f) *smoke*

fumer *to smoke*

fusil (m) *rifle*

G

galerie d'art (f) *art gallery*

gamelle (f) *animal's bowl*

gants (m pl) *gloves*

garage (m) *garage*

garagiste (m) *mechanic*

garantie (f) *guarantee*

garantir *to guarantee*

garçon (m) *boy*; garçon! *waiter!*

gare (f) *station*; gare routière (f) *bus station*

garer *to park*

garniture (f) *filling* (in sandwich, cake)

gâteau (m) *cake*

gauche *left* (not right)

gaz (m) *gas*; gaz à briquet (m) *lighter fluid*

gazoile (m) *diesel*

gel (m) *gel; frost*; gel douche (m) *shower gel*

gênant *embarrassing*

genou (m) *knee*

gens (m pl) *people*

gentil *friendly; kind*

gilet (m) *cardigan*

gin (m) *gin*

gingembre (m) *ginger*

glace (f) *ice; ice cream*

golf (m) *golf*

gomme (f) *eraser*

gorge (f) *throat*

goût (m) *flavour*

goutes (f pl) *drops*

gouttière (f) *gutter*

gouvernement (m) *government*

grand *big; large; tall*; grand magasin (m) *department store*

Grande-Bretagne (f) *Great Britain*

grand-mère (f) *grandmother*

grand-père (m) *grandfather*

grands-parents (m pl) *grandparents*

gras (m) *fat* (on meat, etc)

gratuit *free* (of charge)

grenier (m) *attic*

gril (m) *grill*

grillé(e) *grilled*

gris *grey*

gros, (fem) grosse (adj) *fat*

grotte (f) *cave*

groupe (m) *group*; *band* (musicians)

guêpe (f) *wasp*

guerre (f) *war*

gueule de bois (f) *hangover*

guichet (m) *cashier; ticket office*

guide (m) *guide; guide book*; guide de conversation (m) *phrase book*

guitare (f) *guitar*

H

habituel *ordinary; usual*
hache (f) *axe*
haie (f) *hedge*
hamburger (m) *hamburger*
hamster (m) *hamster*
handicapé *disabled*
haricots (m pl) *beans*
haut *high;* en haut *up;* vers la haut *upwards;* là-haut *up there*
hébergement (m) *accommodation*
hépatite (f) *hepatitis*
herbe (f) *grass*
heure (f) *hour; time*
heures d'ouverture (f pl) *opening times*
heureux *glad; happy*
hier *yesterday*
histoire (f) *history*
hiver (m) *winter*
homard (m) *lobster*
homéopathie *homeopathy*
homme (m) *man*
homosexuel *gay*
honnête *honest*
hôpital (m) *hospital*
horaire (f) *timetable (train, bus)*
horloge (f) *clock*
horrible *horrible*
hors-taxe *duty-free*
hôte (m) *host*
hôtel (m) *hotel*
hôtel de ville (m) *town hall*
hôtesse (f) *hostess;* hôtesse de air *flight attendant*
hoverport (m) *hoverport*
huile (f) *oil*
huit *eight*
huître (f) *oyster*
hydrofoil (m) *hydrofoil*

I

identification (f) *identification*
il *he; it* (m)
île (f) *island;* les îles Anglo-Normandes *Channel Islands*
ils *they* (m); ils sont *they are*
il y a ... *there is/are ...*
immédiatement *immediately*
imperméable (m) *raincoat*
impossible *impossible*
imprimante (f) *printer*
incendie (m) *fire (blaze)*

indigestion (f) *indigestion*
infection (f) *infection*
infirmier, (fem) infirmière *nurse*
information (f) *information*
informations (f pl) *news* (TV)
ingénierie (f) *engineering*
ingénieur (m) *engineer*
inhabituel *unusual*
insecte (m) *insect*
insomnie (f) *insomnia*
instrument de musique (m) *musical instrument*
intelligent *clever*
intéressant *interesting*
internet (m) *internet*
interprète (m) *interpreter*
interpréter *to interpret*
interrupteur (m) *switch*
intoxication alimentaire (f) *food poisoning*
invitation (f) *invitation*
invité(e) *guest*
irlandais(e) *Irish*
Irlande (f) *Ireland*
Italie (f) *Italy*
italien(ne) *Italian*
ivre *drunk*

J

jamais *never*
jambe (f) *leg;* jambe cassée (f) *broken leg*
jambon (m) *ham*
janvier *January*
jardin (m) *garden;* jardin public (m) *park*
jardinerie (f) *garden centre*
jaune *yellow*
jazz (m) *jazz*
je *I;* je suis *I am;* je voudrais *I would like*
jeans (m pl) *jeans*
jeu (m) *game;* jeux vidéos (m pl) *computer games*
jeu de cartes (m) *pack of cards*
jeudi *Thursday*
jeune *young*
joli *nice; pretty* (place etc)
jouer *to play*
jouet (m) *toy*
jour (m) *day*
journal (m) *newspaper*
joyeux anniversaire! *happy birthday!*
juillet *July*

juin *June*
jupe (f) *skirt*
jupon (m) *slip*
jus (m) *juice:* jus d'orange *orange juice;* jus de fruit (m) *fruit juice*
jusqu'à *until*
juste *right; fair (correct);* ce n'est pas juste *it's not fair*
juste un peu *just a little*

K, L

kilo (m) *kilo*
kilomètre (m) *kilometre*
klaxon (m) *horn* (car)
la *the* (fem)
là *there;* il n'est pas là *he's out*
là-bas *over there*
lac (m) *lake*
lacet (m) *shoelace*
laid *ugly*
laine (f) *wool*
laisse (f) *lead*
lait (m) *milk*
lames de rasoir (f pl) *razor blades*
lampe (f) *lamp;* lampe de bureau *reading lamp;* lampe de chevet *bedside lamp;* lampe de poche (f) *torch*
landau (m) *pram*
langouste (f) *crayfish (saltwater)*
langue (f) *language; tongue*
lapin (m) *rabbit*
laque (f) *hairspray*
large *wide*
lavabo (m) *basin (sink)*
laverie automatique (f) *launderette*
lave-vaisselle (m) *dishwasher*
laxatif (m) *laxative*
le *the* (m)
leçon (f) *lesson*
lecteur de cassettes (m) *cassette player*
léger *light* (not heavy)
légumes (m pl) *vegetables*
lent *slow*
lentilles *lenses* (f pl); lentilles rigides *hard lenses;* lentilles semi-souples *gas-permeable lenses;* lentilles souples *soft lenses*
lequel, (fem) laquelle: lequel? *which?;* n'importe lequel *either of them*
les *the* (plural)

lessive (f) *washing powder*

lettre (f) *letter*

leur: leur chambre *their room;* leurs livres *their books*

levée (f) *postal collection*

lever: se lever *to get up*

levier de vitesse (m) *gearstick*

librairie (f) *bookshop*

libre *free (at liberty)*

lime à ongles (f) *nailfile*

limitation de vitesse (f) *speed limit*

limonade (f) *lemonade*

linge (m) *laundry (clothes)*

lingettes (f pl) *baby wipes*

liqueur (f) *liqueur*

liquide: payer en liquide *to pay cash*

lire *to read*

liste (f) *list*

lit (m) *bed;* lit d'enfant (m) *cot*

litérature (f) *literature*

litre (m) *litre*

livraison (f) *delivery*

livre (m) *book;* pound (money, weight)

loin *far*

long, (fem) longue *long*

longueur (f) *length*

lotion solaire (f) *suntan lotion*

louer *to rent*

lourd *heavy*

luge (f) *sled*

lumière (f) *light*

lundi *Monday*

lune (f) *moon;* lune de miel *honeymoon*

lunettes (f pl) *glasses;* lunettes de soleil *sunglasses*

Luxembourg (m) *Luxembourg*

M

ma: ma maison *my house*

machine à laver (f) *washing machine*

maçon (m) *bricklayer*

Madame *Mrs*

Mademoiselle! *waitress!*

magasin (m) *shop;* magasin d'antiquités *antique shop*

magnétoscope (m) *VCR*

mai *May*

maigre *thin*

maillot de bain (m) *swimsuit; swimming trunks*

main (f) *hand*

maintenant *now*

mairie (f) *town hall*

mais *but*

maison (f) *house*

maître de conférences (m) *university lecturer*

malade *ill*

mal à estomac (m) *stomach ache*

mal à la tête (m) *headache*

mal de dents (m) *toothache*

mal de ventre (m) *stomach ache*

manche (f) *sleeve*

Manche: la Manche *Channel*

mandarine (f) *tangerine*

manger *to eat*

manteau (m) *coat*

maquillage (m) *make-up*

marché (m) *market*

marcher *to walk*

mardi *Tuesday*

marée (f) *tide*

margarine (f) *margarine*

mari (m) *husband*

mariage (m) *wedding*

marié *married*

marmelade d'oranges (f) *marmalade*

marron *brown*

mars *March*

marteau (m) *hammer*

mascara (m) *mascara*

mât (m) *mast*

match (m) *match (sport)*

matelas (m) *mattress;* matelas pneumatique *air mattress*

matin (m) *morning*

mauvais *bad; poor* (bad quality); mauvais herbes (f) *weeds*

mécanicien (m) *mechanic*

médecin (m) *doctor*

médicaments (m pl) *medication*

médicine (m) *medicine (subject)*

Méditerranée: la Méditerranée (f) *Mediterranean*

méduse (f) *jellyfish*

meilleur: le meilleur *the best*

melon (m) *melon*

même *same;* le/la même ... *the same ...;* la même chose, s'il vous plaît *the same again, please*

menu (m) *set menu*

mer (f) *sea*

merci *thank you*

mercredi *Wednesday*

mère (f) *mother*

mes: mes chaussures *my shoes*

message (m) *message*

messagerie (f): messagerie électronique *email;* messagerie téléphonique *voicemail*

messe (f) *mass (church)*

métro (m) *underground*

mettre *to put*

meublé *furnished*

meubles (m pl) *furniture*

micro-ondes (m) *microwave*

midday *noon*

miel (m) *honey*

mieux *better*

milieu (m) *middle*

mince *thin*

minuit *midnight*

minute (f) *minute*

miroir (m) *mirror*

mobylette (f) *moped*

mode (f) *fashion*

modem (m) *modem*

moi *me;* c'est moi *it's me;* c'est pour moi; *it's for me;* c'est à moi *it's mine*

moins *less*

mois (m) *month*

mon: mon livre *my book*

moniteur (m) *monitor (computer)*

monnaie (f) *change (money)*

monsieur *sir;* Monsieur *Mr*

montagne (f) *mountain*

montant de tente (m) *tent pole*

monter *to get on (bus etc)*

montre (f) *watch*

monument (m) *monument*

morceau (m) *piece*

mordre *to bite (dog)*

morsure (f) *bite (by dog)*

mort *dead*

mot (m) *word;* mot de passe (m) *password*

moteur (m) *engine (car)*

moto (f) *motorcycle*

mou *soft*

mouche (f) *fly (insect)*

mouchoir (m) *handkerchief*

mouchoirs *tissues*
mouillé *wet*
moules (f pl) *mussels*
mourir *to die*
mousse (f) *mousse (hair)*; mousse à raser (f) *shaving foam*
moustache (f) *moustache*
moustique (m) *mosquito*
moutarde (f) *mustard*
mur (m) *wall (outside)*
mûr *ripe*
mûre (f) *blackberry*
musée (m) *museum*; musée d'art *art gallery*
musicien (m) *musician*; musicien des rues *street musician*
musique (f) *music*; musique classique *classical music*; musique folklorique *folk music*; musique pop *pop music*

N

nager *to swim*
natation (f) *swimming*
navette (pour aéroport) (f) *airport bus*
né(e): je suis né(e) en ... *I was born in ...*
nécessaire *necessary*; ce n'est pas nécessaire *that's not necessary*
négatif (m) *negative (photo)*
négociant en vins (m) *wine merchant*
neige (f) *snow*
neuf *nine*
neuf, (fem) neuve *new*
neveu (m) *nephew*
nez (m) *nose*
ni: ni un ni autre *neither of them*; ni ... ni ... *neither ... nor ...*
nièce (f) *niece*
nier *to deny*
noir *black*
noix (f) *nut (fruit)*
nom (m) *name*; nom de famille (m) *surname*
nombre (m) *number (amount)*
non *no*
nord (m) *north*
nos: nos enfants *our children*
notre: notre maison *our house*
nouer *to tie*
nourriture (f) *food*

nous *we*; nous deux *both of us*; nous sommes *we are*; c'est à nous *it's ours*; c'est nous *it's us*; c'est pour nous *it's for us*
nouveau, (fem) nouvelle *new*; de nouveau *again*
nouvelles (f pl) *news*
novembre *November*
nudiste (m) *nudist*
nuit (f) *night*
nulle part *nowhere*
numéro (m) *number (figure)*

O

objectif (m) *lens (camera)*
objets trouvés (m pl) *lost property*
obturateur (m) *shutter (camera)*
occupé *busy (occupied)*
octobre *October*
odeur (f) *smell*
œil (m) *eye*
œuf (m) *egg*
oignon (m) *onion*
oiseau (m) *bird*
olive (f) *olive*
omelette (f) *omelette*
oncle (m) *uncle*
ondulé *wavy (hair)*
ongle (m) *nail (finger)*
onze *eleven*
opérateur (m) *operator (phone)*
opération (f) *operation*
opticien (m) *optician's*
or (m) *gold*
orage (m) *thunderstorm*
orange (f) *orange (fruit, colour)*
orchestre (m) *orchestra; stalls (theatre)*
ordinateur (m) *computer*; ordinateur portable (m) *laptop*
ordonnance (f) *prescription*
ordre du jour (m) *agenda*
ordures (f pl) *litter; rubbish*
oreille (f) *ear*
oreiller (m) *pillow*
orgue (m) *organ (music)*
os (m) *bone*
ou *or*
où? *where?*
oublier *to forget*

ouest *west*
oui *yes*
ouvert (adj) *open*
ouvre-boîte (m) *can opener*
ouvrir *to open*

P

page (f) *page*
paiement (m) *payment*
pain (m) *bread*; pain grillé (m) *toast*
paire (f) *pair*
palais (m) *palace*
pâle *pale*
palmes (f pl) *flippers*
panier (m) *basket*
panne (f) *breakdown (car)*; je suis tombé en panne *I've had a breakdown*
pansement (m) *plaster*
pantalon (m) *trousers*
pantoufles (f pl) *slippers*
papa *dad*
papier (m) *paper*; papier à lettres *writing paper*; papier cadeau *gift wrap*; papier d'emballage *wrapping paper*; papier filtre *filter paper*; papier hygiénique *toilet paper*
paquet (m) *package, packet*
par: par avion *air mail*; par chemin de fer *by rail*; par exemple *for example*; par nuit *per night*
parapluie (m) *umbrella*
parasol (m) *sunshade*
parce que *because*
parcours de golf (m) *golf course*
pardon!, pardon? *excuse me!; sorry! (apology)*; pardon? *pardon?*
pare-brise (m) *windscreen*
pare-chocs (m) *bumper*
parents (m pl) *parents*
paresseux *lazy*
parfait *perfect*
parfum (m) *perfume*
parking (m) *car park*
parler *to speak, talk*; parlez-vous ...? *do you speak ...?*; je ne parle pas ... *I don't speak*
paroi (f) *wall (inside)*
parterre de fleurs (m) *flowerbed*

parti (m) *party (political)*

particulièrement *especially*

partout *everywhere*

pas *not;* pas beaucoup *not many;* pas encore *not yet;* il n'est pas ... *he's not ...*

passage (m) *driveway*

passager (m) *passenger*

passeport (m) *passport;* passeport d'animaux (m) *pet passport*

passe-temps (m) *hobby*

pastilles pour la gorge (f pl) *throat pastilles*

pâtes (f pl) *pasta*

patinoire (f) *ice rink*

patins à glace (m pl) *ice skates*

pâtisserie (f) *cake shop*

pauvre *poor (not rich)*

payer *to pay*

pays (m) *country (state);* pays de Galles (m) *Wales*

pêche (f) *peach; fishing:* aller à la pêche *to go fishing*

peigne (m) *comb*

peigner *to comb*

peinture (f) *paint; painting*

pelle (f) *spade (shovel)*

pellicule couleur (f) *colour film*

pelouse (f) *lawn*

pendant *during*

pendule (f) *clock*

penser *to think*

pension complète (f) *full board*

père (m) *father*

perle (f) *pearl*

permanente (f) *perm*

permis (m) *licence;* permis de conduire (m) *driving licence*

personne *nobody*

petit *small*

petit ami (m) *boyfriend*

petit déjeuner (m) *breakfast*

petite amie (f) *girlfriend*

petite-fille (f) *granddaughter*

petit-fils (m) *grandson*

petits pois (m pl) *peas*

pétrole (m) *paraffin*

peut-être *maybe; perhaps*

phares (m pl) *headlights*

pharmacie (f) *chemist's*

photo (f) *photograph*

photographe (m/f) *photographer*

photographier *to photograph*

piano (m) *piano*

pickpocket (m) *pickpocket*

pièce (f) *coin; play (theatre)*

pièces de rechange (f pl) *spare parts*

pied (m) *foot*

piéton (m) *pedestrian*

pile (f) *battery (torch)*

pince (f): pince à épiler *tweezers;* pince à linge *peg;* pince à ongles *nail clippers*

pinceau (m) *paintbrush*

pipe (f) *pipe (for smoking)*

pique *spades (cards)*

pique-nique (m) *picnic*

piquer *to bite (snake), sting (insect)*

piquet de tente (m) *tent peg*

piqûre (f) *bite (snake); sting (insect); injection*

pire *worse, worst*

piscine (f) *swimming pool*

piste (f) *runway; ski slope;* piste pour débutants *beginners' slope*

pistolet (m) *pistol*

piston (m) *piston*

pizza (f) *pizza*

placard (m) *cabinet*

place (f) *room (space); seat; square (in town)*

plafond (m) *ceiling*

plage (f) *beach*

plaisanterie (f) *joke*

plan (m) *town map*

plancher (m) *floor (ground)*

plan de travail (m) *worktop*

plancher (m) *floor (ground)*

plante (f) *plant*

plaque d'immatriculation (f) *number plate*

plastique (m) *plastic*

plat *flat (level)*

plateau (m) *tray*

plats (m pl) *main courses;* plats préparés (m pl) *ready meals*

pleurer *to cry (weep)*

plombage (m) *filling (in tooth)*

plombier (m) *plumber*

plongeoir (m) *diving board*

plonger *to dive*

pluie (f) *rain*

plus *more:* plus de *more than;* plus tard *later;* plus ou moins *more or less*

plusieurs *several*

plutôt *quite*

pneu (m) *tyre;* pneu crevé (m) *flat tyre*

poche (f) *pocket*

poêle (f) *frying pan*

poignée (f) *handle (door)*

poignet (m) *wrist*

poire (f) *pear*

poireaux (m) *leek*

poison (m) *poison*

poisson (m) *fish*

poissonnerie (f) *fishmonger's*

poitrine (f) *chest*

poivre (m) *pepper (and salt)*

poivron (m) *pepper (red/green)*

police (f) *police*

policier (m) *police officer*

politique (f) *politics*

pommade (f) *ointment*

pomme (f) *apple*

pomme de terre (f) *potato*

pont (m) *bridge*

porc (m) *pork*

porcelaine (f) *china*

port (m) *harbour; port*

porte (f) *door (building);* porte d'embarquement (f) *gate (at airport)*

porte-bagages (m) *luggage rack*

portefeuille (m) *wallet*

porte-monnaie (m) *purse*

porteur (m) *porter*

portière (f) *car door*

porto (m) *port (drink)*

possible *possible;* dès que possible *as soon as possible*

poste (f) *post; post office*

poster (m) *poster (inside);* (verb) *to post*

pot d'echappement (m) *exhaust (car)*

poubelle (f) *rubbish bin*

poudre (f) *powder*

poulet (m) *chicken*

poupée (f) *doll*

pour *for;* pour moi *for me;* pour une semaine *for a week*

pourboire (m) *tip (money)*

pourquoi? *why?*

pousser *to push*

poussette (f) *pushchair*

pouvoir *to be able;* je peux avoir ...? *can I have ...?;* vous pouvez ...? *can you ...?*

préférer *to prefer*

premier *first;* premier étage (m) *first floor;* première classe *first class;* premiers soins (m pl) *first aid*

prendre *to take;* prendre le train *take the train;* prendre un bain *have a bath*

prénom (m) *first name*

près de *near;* près de la porte *near the door;* près de la fenêtre *by the window*

préservatif (m) *condom*

presque *almost*

pressé: je suis pressé *I'm in a hurry*

pressing (m) *dry cleaner's*

prêt *ready*

prêtre (m) *priest*

prie: je vous en prie *you're welcome*

printemps (m) *spring (season)*

prise (f) *plug (electrical);* prise multiple *adaptor*

prise de sang (f) *blood test*

privé *private*

prix (m) *price;* prix d'entrée *admission charge;* prix du billet (m) *fare*

problème (m) *problem*

prochain *next;* la semaine prochaine *next week*

produit pour la vaisselle (m) *washing-up liquid*

produits de beauté (m pl) *cosmetics*

produits entretien (m pl) *household products*

produits laitiers (m pl) *dairy products*

produits surgelés (m pl) *frozen foods*

professeur (m) *professor; teacher (secondary)*

profession (f) *profession*

profond *deep*

promener: aller se promener *to go for a walk*

propre (adj) *clean*

prudent *careful;* soyez prudent! *be careful!*

public (m) *public*

puce (f) *flea*

pull (m) *sweater*

punaise (f) *drawing pin*

pyjama (m) *pyjamas*

Q

quai (m) *dock; platform*

qualité (f) *quality*

quand? *when?*

quarante *forty*

quart (m) *quarter*

quatorze *fourteen*

quatre *four*

quatre-vingt *eighty*

quatre-vingt-dix *ninety*

quatrième *fourth*

que *than*

quel âge avez-vous? *how old are you?*

quelle heure est-il? *what's the time?*

quelque chose *something*

quelque part *somewhere*

quelquefois *sometimes*

quelqu'un *somebody*

quelqu'un d'autre *someone else*

qu'est-ce que c'est? *what's that?; what is it?*

question (f) *question*

queue (f) *queue*

qui? *who?*

quincaillerie (f) *hardware shop*

quinze *fifteen;* quinze jours *fortnight*

R

radiateur (m) *heater; radiator*

radio (f) *x-ray; radio*

radis (m) *radish*

rafraîchissements (m pl) *refreshments*

raie (f) *parting (in hair)*

raisin (m) *grape;* raisin sec (m) *raisin*

rallonge (f) *extension lead*

ramer *to row*

rames (f pl) *oars*

randonée (f) *hiking*

rapide *fast; quick*

rapport de police (m) *police report*

rare *rare (uncommon)*

raser: se raser *to shave*

rat (m) *rat*

râteau (m) *rake*

rayon (m) *aisle (supermarket)*

réception (f) *reception*

receptionniste (m/f) *receptionist*

réclamation de bagages (f) *baggage claim*

recommandé: en recommandé *registered post*

record (m) *record (sports etc)*

reçu (m) *receipt*

réduction (f) *discount*

regarde: cela ne vous regarde pas *it's none of your business*

regarder *to watch*

règle (f) *ruler*

rein (m) *kidney*

religion (f) *religion*

remercier *to thank*

remonte-pente (m) *ski lift*

remorque (f) *trailer*

rendez-vous (m) *appointment*

rendre *to return (give back);* rendre visite *visit (person)*

repas (m) *meal*

repasser *to iron*

répondeur (m) *answering machine*

reposer: se reposer *to rest (relax)*

reseignments (m pl) *directory (telephone)*

réservation (f) *reservation*

réserver *to book, reserve*

résistant *strong (material)*

respirer *to breathe*

ressort (m) *spring (mechanical)*

restaurant (m) *restaurant*

reste (m) *rest (remainder)*

retard (m) *delay*

retirer *to withdraw*

rétroviseur (m) *car mirror*

réunion (f) *meeting*

réveil (m) *alarm clock*

revenir *to return (come back)*

revue (f) *magazine*

rez-de-chaussée (m) *ground floor*

rhum (m) *rum*

rhume (m) *cold (illness);* rhume des foins (m) *hay fever*

riche *rich*

rideau (m) *curtain*

rien *nothing*; ça ne fait rien *it doesn't matter*

rire *to laugh*

rivière (f) *river*

riz (m) *rice*

robe (f) *dress*

robinet (m) *tap (water)*

rocher (m) *rock (stone)*

rock (m) *rock (music)*

roman (m) *novel*

rond *round (circular)*

rondelle (f) *washer*

rond-point (m) *roundabout*

room service (m) *room service*

rose (f) *rose; pink* (adj)

rôti *roasted*

roue (f) *wheel*

rouge *red*; rouge à lèvres (m) *lipstick*

rougeur (f) *rash*

rouleaux (m pl) *curlers*

roux *red (of hair)*

rue (f) *street*

rugby (m) *rugby*

ruines (f pl) *ruins*

ruisseau (m) *stream (small river)*

S

sa: sa maison *his/her house*

sable (m) *sand*

sac (m) *bag*; sac à dos *backpack*; sac à main *handbag*; sac de couchage *sleeping bag*; sac poubelle *bin liner*

saignant *rare (steak)*

salade (f) *lettuce; salad*

salle (f) *room*; salle à manger *dining room*; salle d'attente *waiting room*; salle d'opérations *operating theatre*; salle de bains *bathroom*; salle de conférences *conference room*; salle de radiology *x-ray departement*; salle des urgences *emergency departement*

salon (m) *living room*

salut *hi*

samedi *Saturday*

sandales (f pl) *sandals*

sandwich (m) *sandwich*

sang (m) *blood*

sans *without*; sans plomb *unleaded*

santé! *cheers!*

s'arrêter *to stop*

sauce (f) *sauce*

saucisse (f) *sausage*

saumon (m) *salmon*

sauna (m) *sauna*

savoir *to know* (fact); je ne sais pas *I don't know*

savon (m) *soap*

science (f) *science*

seau (m) *bucket*

sec, (fem) sèche *dry*

sèche-cheveux (m) *hairdryer*

seconde (f) *second (of time)*

seconde: en seconde *second class*

secrétaire (m/f) *secretary*

secteur (m) *field (academic)*

sécurité: en sécurité *safe (not in danger)*

seize *sixteen*

sel (m) *salt*

semaine (f) *week*

séminaire (m) *seminar*

sentir *to smell*

séparé (adj) *separate*

séparer *to separate*

sept *seven*

septembre *September*

sérieux *serious*

seringue (f) *syringe*

séropositif(ve) *HIV positive*

serveur (m) *waiter*

serveuse (f) *waitress*

service de pédiatrie (m) *children's ward*

serviette (f) *towel*

serviettes hygiéniques (f pl) *sanitary towels*

ses: ses chaussures *his/her shoes*

seul *alone; single (one)*

seulement *only*

shampooing (m) *shampoo*

short (m) *shorts*

si *if; whether*

SIDA *AIDS*

siège pour bébé (m) *car seat (for a baby)*

siège social (m) *head office*

silencieux *quiet (person)*

s'il vous plaît *please*

simple *simple*

sirop (m) *syrup*

site web (m) *web site*

six *six*

ski (m) *ski*; faire du ski *to go skiing*

skier *to ski*

slip (m) *underpants*

snack (m) *snack*

sœur(f) *sister*

soie (f) *silk*

soif: j'ai soif *I'm thirsty*

soir (m) *evening*; ce soir *tonight*

soirée (f) *party (get together)*

soit ... soit ... *either ... or ...*

soixante *sixty*

soixante-dix *seventy*

soldes (f pl) *sale (at reduced prices)*

soleil (m) *sun*

solution de trempage (f) *soaking solution (for contact lenses)*

sommeil (m) *sleep*

somnifère (m) *sleeping pill*

son livre *his/her book*

sonnette (f) *bell (door)*

sortie (f) *exit*

sortie de secours (f) *emergency exit*

sortir *to leave*

soucoupe (f) *saucer*

soûl *drunk*

soupape (f) *valve*

soupe (f) *soup*

souper (m) *supper*

sourcil (m) *eyebrow*

sourd *deaf*

sourire (m) *smile; smile* (verb)

souris (f) *mouse*

sous ... *below ...; under ...*

sous-sol (m) *basement*

sous-vêtements (f pl) *underwear*

soutien-gorge (m) *bra*

souvenir (m) *souvenir; remember* (verb); je m'en souviens *I remember*; je ne me souviens pas *I don't remember*

souvent *often*

sport(m) *sport*

stade (m) *stadium*

stagiaire (m) *trainee*

station (f) *underground station*

station de ski (f) *ski resort*

station-service (f) *petrol station*

statue (f) *statue*

steak (m) *steak*

store (m) *blind (window)*

stupide *stupid*

stylo (m) *pen*; stylo-bille (m) *ballpoint pen*; stylo-plume (m) *fountain pen*

sucette (f) *lollipop*

sucre (m) *sugar*

sucré *sweet (not sour)*

sud(m) *south*

suisse(sse) *Swiss*

Suisse: la Suisse *Switzerland*

supermarché (m) *supermarket*

supplément (m) *supplement*

suppositoire (m) *suppository*

sur ... *on ...*

sûr *sure*

survêtement (m) *track suit*

sweat-shirt (m) *sweatshirt*

sympathique *nice* (person)

synagogue (f) *synagogue*

syndicat d'initiative (m) *tourist office*

T

ta: ta maison *your house* (singular informal)

tabac (m) *tobacco; tobacconist*

table (f) *table*

tablette de chocolat (f) *bar of chocolate*

taille (f) *size*

taille-crayon (m) *pencil sharpener*

talc (m) *talcum powder*

talon (m) *heel*

tampon (m) *tampon*

tante (f) *aunt*

tapis (m) *carpet;* tapis de sol (m) *groundsheet*

tapisserie (f) *tapestry*

tard *late;* bus est en retard *the bus is late*

tasse (f) *cup; mug*

taux de change (m) *exchange rate*

taxi (m) *taxi*

télé cablée (f) *cable TV*

téléphérique (m) *cable car*

téléphone (m) *telephone;* téléphone portable (m) *mobile phone*

téléphoner *to telephone* (verb)

télévision (f) *television*

témoin (m) *witness*

température (f) *temperature*

tempête (f) *storm;* tempête de neige (f) *blizzard*

temps (m) *weather; time;* de temps en temps *occasionally*

tennis (m) *tennis;* les tennis (m pl) *trainers*

tente (f) *tent*

terminal (m) *terminal*

terrain de camping (m) *campsite*

terrasse (f) *terrace*

terre (f) *land; soil*

tes: tes chaussures *your shoes* (singular informal; plural noun)

tête (f) *head*

thé (m) *tea*

théâtre (m) *theatre*

ticket (m) *ticket* (underground, bus)

timbre (m) *stamp*

tire-bouchon (m) *corkscrew*

tirer *to pull*

tiroir (m) *drawer*

tissu (m) *material*

toboggan (m) *toboggan*

toi: c'est à toi *it's yours*

toilettes (f pl) *toilets*

toit (m) *roof*

tomate (f) *tomato*

ton: ton livre *your book* (singular informal)

tondeuse à gazon (f) *lawn mower*

tongs (f pl) *flip-flops*

tonic (m) *tonic*

torchon (m) *dish cloth*

tôt *early*

toucher *to feel, touch*

toujours *always*

tour (f) *tower*

tourism (m) *sightseeing*

touriste (m/f) *tourist*

tourne-disque (m) *record player*

tournevis (m) *screwdriver*

tous les deux *both of them*

tousser *to cough*

tout *all; everything;* tout droit *straight on;* tout le monde *everyone;* tout seul *all alone*

toux (f) *cough*

tracteur (m) *tractor*

tradition (f) *tradition*

traducteur (m) *translator*

traduire *to translate*

train (m) *train*

tranquille *quiet* (street, etc.)

transpiration (f) *sweat*

transpirer *to sweat*

travail (m) *job; work*

travailler *to work*

traverser *to cross over*

trèfle *clubs* (cards)

treize *thirteen*

trente *thirty*

très *very*

tricoter *knit*

triste *sad*

trois *three*

troisième *third*

trop *too* (excessively)

trottoir (m) *pavement*

tu *you* (singular informal); tu es *you are*

tunnel (m) *tunnel;* le tunnel sous La Manche *Channel Tunnel*

tuyau (m) *pipe* (for water)

U

un/une *a; one;* un/une autre *another* (different)

université (f) *university*

urgence (f) *emergency*

urgent *urgent*

utensiles de cuisine (f pl) *cooking utensils*

utile *useful*

utiliser *to use*

V

vacances (m pl) *holiday*

vaccination (f) *vaccination*

vague (f) *wave; faint* (adj)

valise (f) *case*

valise (f) *suitcase*

vallée (f) *valley*

vanille (f) *vanilla*

vapeur: à la vapeur *steamed*

vase (m) *vase*

veau (m) *veal*

végétarien (adj) *vegetarian*

véhicule (m) *vehicle*

vélo (m) *bicycle;* vélo tout terrain (m) *mountain bike*

vendre *to sell*

vendredi *Friday*

venir *to come;* je viens de ... *I come from ...*

vent (m) *wind*

vente (f) *sale* (transaction)

ventilateur (m) *fan* (ventilator)

vernis à ongles (m) *nail polish*

verre (m) *glass*

verres de contact (f pl) *contact lenses*

verrou (m) *bolt* (on door)

verrouiller *to bolt*

vert *green*

veste (f) *jacket*

vêtements (m pl) *clothes*

vétérinaire (m) *vet*
viande (f) *meat*
vide *empty*
vidéo (f) *video*
  (film/tape)
vie (f) *life*
vieux, (fem) vieille *old*
villa (f) *villa*
village (m) *village*
ville (f) *city; town*
vin (m) *wine*
vinaigre (m) *vinegar*
vingt *twenty*
violet *purple*
violon (m) *violin*
vis (f) *screw*
visage (m) *face*
viseur (m) *viewfinder*
visite (f) *tour; visit*
visiter *to visit* (place)
visiteur (m) *visitor*
vitesse (f) *gear* (car);
  speed

vodka (f) *vodka*
voile (f) *sailing*
voilier (m) *sailing boat*
voir *to see;* je vois *I see;*
  je ne vois rien *I can't*
  see anything
voiture (f) *car; train*
  carriage
voix(f) *voice*
vol (m) *flight*
volaille (f) *poultry*
volant (m) *steering*
  wheel
voler *to fly; steal;* on a
  volé *it's been stolen*
volet (m) *shutter*
  (window)
voleur (m) *thief*
vomir *to be sick* (vomit)
vos: vos chaussures
  your shoes (singular
  formal; plural;
  plural noun)

votre: votre maison *your*
  house (singular
  formal; plural;
  singular noun)
vouloir *to want;* je veux
  I want; vous voulez?
  do you want?
vous *you* (singular
  formal; plural); vous
  êtes *you are*
voyage (m) *journey*
vrai *true*
vue (f) *view*

W, Y, Z

wagon-lit (m) *sleeper*
wagon-restaurant (m)
  restaurant car
whisky (m) *whisky*
yaourt (m) *yoghurt*
yeux (m pl) *eyes*
zoo (m) *zoo*

Acknowledgments

The publisher would like to thank the following for their help in the preparation of this book: Anne-Marie Miller for the organization of location photography in France; Hôtel-Restaurant, "Le Rabelais", Fontenay le Comte; Gare Routière de Fontenay le Comte; Pharmacie Parot, Nieul Sur L'Autise; Garage Gouband, Oulmes; Musée de l'Abbaye de Nieul Sur L'Autise (Cabinet Tetrac, Nantes); Boulangerie des familles, Coulon; Fromagerie, rue St Marthe, Niort; Fruits et Primeurs Benoit, Halles de Niort; Gare SNCF de Niort; Magnet Showroom, Enfield, MyHotel, London; Kathy Gammon; Juliette Meeus and Harry.

Language content for Dorling Kindersley by G-AND-W PUBLISHING
Managed by **Jane Wightwick**
Editing and additional input: **Pamela Wightwick, Christine Arthur, Leila Gaafar**

Additional design assistance: **Lee Riches, Fehmi Cömert, Sally Geeve**
Additional editorial assistance: **Paul Docherty, Lynn Bresler**
Picture research: **Louise Thomas**

Picture credits

Key:
t=top; *b*=bottom; *l*=left, *r*=right; *c*=centre; *A*=above; *B*=below

p2 **Alamy:** *Ian Dagnall cr;* *p4/5* **Alamy:** *f1 Online tl; images-of-france tr;* **Alamy RF:** *Andy Marshall bl;* **DK Images:** *br; Neil Lukas tcr;* *p6/7* **Laura Knox:** *cl;* *p10/12* **Alamy RF:** *BananaStock cAr; RubberBall cBl;* **Ingram Image Library:** *bl;* *p12/13* **Alamy RF:** *John Foxx cAr; RubberBall br;* **DK Images:** *cl; Steve Shott cBr;* **Ingram Image Library:** *tr, cr;* *p14/15* **Alamy:** *images-of-france tcr;* **Ingram Image Library:** *cAl, cl, cBl, cAr, cBr, bcr;* *p16/17* **Alamy RF:** *RubberBall br;* **Ingram Image Library:** *tr;* *p18/19* **DK Images:** *David Murray tr; Ian O'Leary clB;* *p22/23* **DK Images:** *cl, Andy Crawford cAr; Susanna Price br; Magnus Rew tcrB;* **Ingram Image Library:** *bcl, tcr;* *p24/25* **DK Images:** *cA, Dave King tcr;* *p26/27* **Ingram Image Library:** *cl;* *p28/29* **DK Images:** *Andy Crawford tcr; Dave King cr; Matthew Ward bclA;* **Ingram Image Library:** *bcrA, bcr; p30/31* **Alamy RF:** *Comstock Images bcl;* **DK Images:** *cl, bclA;* *p36/37* **DK Images:** *bcl; bcr; Magnus Rew cl;* **Ingram Image Library:** *bl;* *p38/39* **Alamy RF:** *Imageshop / Zefa Visual Media cl;* *p40/41* **Alamy:** *images-of-france bl;* **Alamy RF:** *Justin Kase cAr;* **DK Images:** *cl, bcr;* *p42/43* **Alamy:** *Artografika Bildagentur cr;* **Alamy RF:** *Image Source tcr, cAr; Andy Marshall cAAr;* *p44/45* Courtesy of **Renault:** *cl;* *p46/47* **Alamy:** *Artografika Bildagentur cr; images-of-france cl;* **Alamy RF:** *Imageshop / Zefa Visual Media br;* **DK Images:** *bcl;* **Ingram Image Library:** *trlB; Courtesy of* **Renault:** *tcr;* *p48/49* **Alamy:** *Agence Images tcr; Ian Dagnell cr; PCL bcr; Peter Titmuss cr;* **DK Images:** *bcl;* *p50/51* **Alamy:** *Robert Harding Picture Library c;* *p52/53* **Alamy:** *imagebroker tcr;* **Alamy RF:** *Image Farm Inc cAr; Photov.com / Hisham Ibrahim tcrB;* **DK Images:** *cl;* *p54/55* **Alamy:** *Frank Herholdt bcl; Jackson Smith cBl;* **Alamy RF:** *BananaStock cl; John Foxx c; Image Source cAr; ThinkStock bl;* **DK Images:** *Andy Crawford bclA;* *p56/57* **Alamy:** *Agence Images clA; Ian Dagnell cl; PCL tl; Peter Titmuss cAl;* **DK Images:** *clAA,* Courtesy of **Renault:** *bc;* *p58/59* **Alamy:** *Michael Juno tcr;* **Alamy RF:** *Brand X Pictures cBl, cBBl; Image Source cAAl;* **DK Images:** *cAl;* *p60/61* **Alamy:** *Robert Harding Picture Library bcr;* **Alamy RF:** *Image Source cAr;* **DK Images:** *Steve Gorton bl, tcrB; Pia Tryde cAAr;* **Ingram Image Library:** *tr;* *p62/63* **DK Images:** *Stephen Whitehorn cl;* *p64/65* **Alamy:** *Arcaid bcrA;* **Alamy RF:** *GKPhotography cBr; Goodshoot cAAr; imagebroker c; Justin Kase tcrB;* **DK Images:** *Steve Tanner cAr;* **Ingram Image Library:** *tcr;* *p66/67* **Alamy:** *Arcaid tl;* **Alamy RF:** *Image Source cAr;* **DK Images:** *tr; Stephen Whitehorn bl;* **Ingram Image Library:** *br;* *p68/69* **Alamy:** *Balearic Pictures cr; f1 Online cBl; Doug Houghton cl; Indiapicture clB;* **Alamy RF:** *images-of-france cBr; Justin Kase bl;* **DK Images:** *Peter Wilson cAl;* *p72/73* **Alamy RF:** *imagebroker tcrB; Image Source cAr; Comstock Images bl;* **Alamy RF:** *Doug Norman bl;* **Ingram Image Library:** *c;* *p76/77* **Alamy:** *Balearic Pictures cBl; f1 Online clB; Indiapicture bl;* **Alamy RF:** *Peter Wilson bcl;* *p80/81* **Getty:** *Taxi / Rob Melnychuk br;* **Ingram Image Library:** *cr; Xerox UK Ltd:* *tcr;* *p82/83* **Alamy:** *wildphotos.com tcr;* **Alamy RF:** *FogStock cAAl; Momentum Creative Group cl; Shoosh / Up the Res cBl;* **Ingram Image Library:** *cl;* *p84/85* **Alamy:** *Brand X Pictures cr; f1 Online c;* **Alamy RF:** *BananaStock bl; SuperStock tr;* **Ingram Image Library:** *crB;* *p86/87* **Getty:** *Taxi / Rob Melnychuk tc;* *p90/91* **Alamy RF:** *Brand X Pictures tcr;* **DK Images:** *cl; David Jordan cAr; Stephen Oliver cr;* **Ingram Image Library:** *cBr;* *p92/93* **Alamy RF:** *Pixland cr;* **DK Images:** *cl; Guy Ryecart tr;* *p94/95* **Alamy:** *David Kamm cl; Phototake Inc bcl;* **Alamy RF:** *Comstock Images cr; ImageState Royalty Free bcr;* **DK Images:** *Stephen Oliver tcr;* *p96/97* **Alamy RF:** *Pixland br;* **DK Images:** *tl;* **Ingram Image Library:** *cr;* *p98/99* **Alamy RF:** *Bildagentur Franz Waldhaeusl bl; ThinkStock br;* **DK Images:** *Peter Kindersley cr;* **Getty RF:** *Photodisc Green c;* *p102/103* **Alamy:** *The Garden Picture Library tcr; cAr; Hortus b; D Hurst tcrB;* **Ingram Image Library:** *cAr;* *p104/105* **DK Images:** *Paul Bricknell cl(6); Jane Burton bcl; Geoff Dann cl(2); Max Gibbs cl(4); Frank Greenaway cl(3); Dave King cl(1), cAr; Tracy Morgan cl(5);* *p106/107* **Alamy:** *The Garden Picture Library br;* **DK Images:** *Peter Kindersley cr;* *p110/111* **Alamy RF:** *RubberBall cr;* **DK Images:** *Andy Crawford cl;* *p112/113* **Alamy RF:** *Image Source cl;* **DK Images:** *bl;* **Ingram Image Library:** *tcr, bcr;* *p114/115* **Alamy:** *FogStock tcr; David R Frazier Photolibrary, Inc cBr;* **Alamy RF:** *Image Source cAr; Index Stock cAl;* **DK Images:** *Max Alexander cr;* *p116/117* **Alamy:** *The Garden Picture Library cAl;* *p118/119* **DK Images:** *Steve Gorton tlr;* **GettyNews:** *Giuseppe Cacace c;* *p121* **Alamy:** *ImageState / Pictor International cl;* **Alamy RF:** *Sarkis Images cr;* **DK Images:** *cBl, bcl; Kevin Mallett br;* *p122/123* **Alamy:** *BananaStock cA;* **Ingram Image Library:** *cl;* *p124/125* **Alamy:** *ImageState / Pictor International bclA;* **DK Images:** *cBl, bcl; Paul Bricknell tc(5); Geoff Dann tc(3); Max Gibbs tc(1); Frank Greenaway tc(2); Dave King tc(4); Kevin Mallett bl; Tracy Morgan tc(6);* *p126/127* **Alamy:** *imagebroker clB;* **Alamy RF:** *© Hisham Ibrahim / Photov.com blA; Image Farm Inc bl;* *p128* **DK Images:** *Neil Mersh.*

All other images **Mike Good.**